From Fear to Success

A Practical Public-speaking Guide

Thomas B. Dowd III

Contents

Contents continued

PART I

The Public-speaking Beast

1.

Step into the Public Forum

My first memory of public speaking was in the fourth grade. I was asked to present some topic that I can't even recall in front of a class of about twenty students. What I remember is the heat running up to my face and head, and the heart palpitations that caused greater tension and fear as I walked to the front of the room. After what I remember to be a dreadful display of public speaking, I became disoriented. I walked down the wrong aisle and sat down in someone else's seat.

This frightful performance was followed a few years later as I awaited my turn to present to my seventh-grade class. I misread the ending of a classmate's presentation and prematurely went to the front of the room. Not knowing what to do, I sat frozen on the desk beside her while she spent the next five minutes finishing her thoughts. I was dumbfounded, and could only hope the entire class could not see the panic running through me from my mistake, all the while dreading the embarrassing performance to come.

I could go on with many other stories that show my own failure in the public forum. Instead of focusing on the paralyzing potential of the public speaking world in this book, I will share with you the observations and lessons that have taught me to be a confident and successful speaker. I want to teach you how to change the fear that freezes so many of us into positive energy so that you can not only survive a public-speaking experience, but can gain the confidence needed to *want* to share your message with others.

Public-speaking fear emerges early on, as childhood inhibitions slowly turn to hesitation and angst. We'll discuss some of these sources of stage fright shortly. We each have our individual reasons for why stepping in front of a group of people becomes so daunting. I know firsthand the physical and mental anguish of stepping into a public forum when my words became gibberish and my thoughts left my mind. I have had to work hard to gain control of my faculties to be able to successfully share thoughts, feelings, and stories in such a way that people want to listen to me. Shockingly, I can't wait to do it now. This learned confidence has made me successful both personally and professionally.

As a public speaker and author, I have taken the lessons and observations that have worked for me and turned them into practical tips that speakers at all levels can use. My approach teaches hands-on, realistic applications that can be implemented right away. I can't say that it's not as hard as it looks to stand in front of a group of people, but I can say that implementing the information in this book will make the experience easier, and—believe it or not—even enjoyable.

In this age of headline news and information overload, who has time to read a book on public speaking? We decide we will work on these skills later, when we have more time. Maybe simply avoiding the topic will somehow make the fear go away. Be aware: it is not a matter of *if* you will have to speak in public; it is a matter of *when*. Will you have to give a Thanksgiving dinner toast? Will you have to make a cold sale to a new potential client? Do you have a burning question as an audience member, but are too scared to ask it? Are you sitting at a cocktail party or at a business networking event where you don't know anyone and are paralyzed against a wall?

There are plenty of books on this subject, ranging from an academic approach diagnosing physical and mental barriers that cause stage fright to guidance on becoming a professional speaker. This book won't show you how to perform academic research on what's going on in our body and head, or how to break into the speaking profession. I realize that everyone's motives for improvement will vary. My intentions are to provide speakers of all levels with the foundation to give them the courage to take action to develop and grow. The fact that you picked up this book is a good indicator that you want to improve.

My approach is straightforward. Let me intentionally repeat myself: my approach is straightforward. Let's break down the fundamentals of practical public speaking. You will be ahead of the game if you take nothing more out of this book than the following:

1. Effective public speaking is more about confidence than communication skills.
2. Public speaking is more than a lectern, podium, or microphone; it is everywhere.
3. The ability to speak publicly is not as hard as you may imagine—the hardest part is taking the first action steps.
4. Public speaking is a learned skill that must continually be developed.
5. Your own success, both personal and professional, is directly related to your ability to communicate effectively.

These fundamentals will permeate the suggestions and recommendations throughout this book.

Most people I have coached through public speaking already have some communication skills. Skill levels vary by individual. Many of them can have what seems like a normal conversation in person or over the phone, until they hear the phrase "public speaking." I have seen a roomful of people freeze in horror when they are asked to step up front to provide a one-minute introduction. Here is a key lesson: speak of something that you know or that relates to you. Whether you are asked to give a quick introduction or a full keynote speech, integrate familiar stories into the presentation. Why? Because you know yourself better than anyone else does, which should make you more comfortable. This fact alone should give you a small dose of confidence that you know what will be coming out of your mouth next.

Although the majority of references in this book involve public speaking, many of the road blocks to successful speaking are not about the speaking portion of communication at all. We can all improve our ability to formulate a thought and then express it; however, a large hurdle people run into is *confidence*. How can you gain confidence? Having someone tell you that you need to increase your confidence is like having someone tell you to relax when you are tense. It's not easy, but there are specific steps we can take to become more confident.

Confidence can be gained through preparation, practice, and repetition. The fact that you are familiar with the material you are about to present should be a powerful boost. Every time you do some form of public speaking, a little bit of discomfort or anxiety goes away. Look for small wins. You may not notice the gains immediately, and the discomfort may not go away completely, but you *will* start to realize that you are improving. If you want proof, simply videotape yourself for a week. Give a short prepared speech (length is not relevant). Tape the presentation each day for a week. I can promise you that you will see improvements that will bring a smile to your face. Imagine taking that feeling over weeks and months and years. Find ways to knock down your personal barriers one step at a time, and turn your uncomfortable situations into manageable situations that will result in greater confidence.

Not everyone is scrambling to jump behind a lectern (unless it's to hide) or command a stage to extend a message. Have you ever run into someone in the hall at work? Have you ever been interviewed? Have you ever been in a business presentation where you were asked a question and needed a quick response? Everyday situations surround us where, if we had confidence in ourselves, we could turn our fear into success. Don't fool yourself into thinking that you can avoid public communication. Your success is often directly aligned with your ability to confidently present yourself.

It is obviously a fact that we are surrounded with everyday interactions that can change the perceptions we have about ourselves, and the perceptions other people have about us. Imagine taking action on your desire to improve your confidence; you can do anything you set your sights on. You can be the person, communicator, and leader you want to be. Your improved confidence and skills can translate into promotions, better interpersonal relationships, or just about any other goals you've set.

As someone constantly on the go with work and life, I have often felt I didn't have the time to address my public speaking shortcomings. I was too busy in the daily grind to lift my head up enough to see that if I improved my communication skills and confidence, I could improve other things like my leadership and time-management skills. For example, when I managed a team of about fifteen people, I constantly found myself answering the same questions over and over, or repeating myself. I learned to confidently convey messages and expectations that were clear, concise, and actionable. Guess what? I found myself saving time by not repeating myself, and more importantly, started to see people taking the actions to be autonomous because they started to believe in themselves. I began to believe that I had the ability to inspire others.

Improving yourself is not as hard as you think. The fact that you want to improve is a huge step. I chose to join Toastmasters International. Toastmasters is a proven method to improve communication and leadership skills with approximately 270,000 members in 13,000 clubs worldwide. Their mission statement reads:

"The mission of a Toastmasters club is to provide a mutually supportive and positive learning environment in which every individual member has the opportunity to develop oral communication and leadership skills, which in turn foster self-confidence and personal growth."

Joining Toastmasters is not a prerequisite or the only way to improve public-speaking skills, but it is a methodical approach to self-paced learning in an encouraging environment.

Before you start your journey, have a goal in mind. Obviously this goal will evolve, but you need a starting point. When you reach this goal, set another, slightly higher goal. For example, if you simply want to confidently read a story to kids in the library, then keep working toward it. You can start reading in front of a mirror to yourself. Once you are comfortable, ask family and friends to listen to you. After you are comfortable with them, then you can go to the library, ready to read to the kids. You are surrounded with opportunities; you simply have to cross the threshold.

From Fear to Success

Crossing the threshold to take action is hard only if you are holding yourself back. I worked with an individual to improve her confidence level in order to be able to lead her team of twenty people in a daily morning meeting. When I suggested joining Toastmasters, she said she'd been thinking about it for a long time. The next natural question was, "Why not join now?" I heard the same excuses and comments I hear far too often: *I don't have the time, I need to work it into my schedule,* or *I have it on my to-do list.* That to-do list is not getting any shorter, nor is it getting enough action. I gently pressed on to say that the improvement happens only when the person is ready to take the action to improve. Her completed Toastmasters application was on my desk a couple of hours later. She is now on her way to becoming more successful.

These practical tips are intended to be a reference guide for you. This book isn't about staying ahead of the curve with what's hot (I like to call it flavor-of-the-day business jargon), or creating and using buzz words. This is about the fundamental tools of public speaking. The tools referenced will remain timeless.

I would be naïve to say that communications have not advanced. We have evolved to different communication channels, from rotary phones to "smart phones" where we can "tweet" our own message to hundreds, thousands, or millions of people at once, to webinars as a way of public speaking. What will remain constant, however, is the need to communicate our messages clearly and confidently. No matter what the means of communication are, we still need these critical skills.

Public speaking is a learned skill that can and should be developed, refined, and honed. I do not believe that some people have it and some people don't. *Everyone* can pick up these skills. As with most things, the more you do it, the more comfortable and successful you will be. Public speaking is a learned skill that needs nurturing.

Not all chapters in this book will be relevant to your speaking evolution at the same time. However, as you grow with your skills and abilities, different chapters will meet your evolving needs and timing. The information will show you how and what to do to make a difference personally and professionally. The tips are easy to follow and easy to implement. Exercising your public-speaking abilities will stimulate your whole being until these abilities become locked into your inner core. Despite what you may have heard, public speaking shouldn't be scarier than death. Public speaking is a skill waiting to be harnessed *before* your death. Congratulations. You are about to start your journey to success.

2.

Find the Sources of Stage Fright

You are approaching the lectern for the "big" presentation, or you're about to have the interview that will change the course of your life. You get dizzy; your heart pounds; your mouth gets dry. It seems to happen every time you need most to be calm, cool, and collected! What if you understood the root causes of your stage fright and anxiety? Understanding the sources of stage fright will enable you, the potential speaker, to take the steps necessary to address the fright head-on. The choice is fight or flight. It's time to fight back and get you to be the calm, cool, collected person you can be.

Make the anxiety go away. It may not be possible to make it go away fully, but wouldn't you like to have command over these feelings so you can take advantage of the opportunities presented to you? Stage fright can be categorized as biological, psychological, social, cultural, or a combination of all of the above. Some people might stop reading here, and say that there is far too much to go through to "solve" the public-speaking anxiety, so maybe avoiding it altogether is the best course of action.

I wish it was that easy. Depending on your job, for example, it may be a little easier to avoid these situations. However, what happens when you're asked to be the best man or maid of honor in a wedding?

What if you are forced into the unfortunate duty of delivering a close friend's eulogy? What if you want to buy a car and need to negotiate? It should be becoming clear that avoiding public speaking situations isn't as easy as you might think, because they are everywhere. When you learn to address the symptoms straight on rather than avoiding the situation entirely, you will find that each new situation will get a little easier. Your confidence level will skyrocket. You may not notice it right away, but the invested time to practice and prepare will pay off in the end.

Can you "unlearn" the pent-up fears that have kept you from being your best? My wife often notes that I've successfully untrained everything she has taught our dog. Therefore, I have to believe we can turn the tides on our own emotions and confidence level.

I know what you're thinking: Can't you just give me medication? Is there an "app" for that? In a culture where we are constantly looking for a quick fix, they are available. If you do a search on iTunes, for example, it will bring up podcasts and applications relating to the topic of public speaking and stage fright. As far as medication, some jokingly may say, "Have a drink." I have read many books and articles on public speaking that reference the use of alcohol to calm nerves. All have very clearly stated the obvious risk of overindulgence, when you go beyond the calming of nerves you begin to impact your ability to think and speak clearly.

There are similar risks associated with taking medications, which only conceal the symptoms for a little while. You must remember that public speaking is everywhere, so reaching for medication may suffice for that one-time event, but may not always be there for a chance meeting that can change your life. The website www.changethatsrightnow.com

was one of many sources offering tips for quick resolutions to stage fright. There are many medications suggested to combat anxiety and stage fright. The organization Change That's Right Now describes the following three medications:

"Beta blockers are used for relieving performance anxiety. They work by blocking the flow of adrenaline that occurs when you're anxious. While beta blockers don't affect the emotional symptoms of anxiety, they can control physical symptoms such as shaking hands or voice, sweating, and rapid heartbeat.

"Antidepressants can be helpful when the feelings of fear are severe and debilitating. Three specific antidepressants — Paxil, Effexor, and Zoloft — have been approved by the U.S. Food and Drug Administration phobias.

"Benzodiazepines are fast-acting anti-anxiety medications. However, they are sedating and addictive, so they are typically prescribed only when other medications have not worked."

As with any discussion about medication, please check with your doctor before taking it to fully understand the impact it may have on your mind and body.

My caution for these suggestions—besides the side effects that may take some television commercials far too long to disclose to meet the regulations, at least in the United States—is the fact that the taking of this medication does not get to the root cause of the issue. Drugs are for short-term solutions. In fact, I think solution is probably too strong a word. I think it should actually be *mask* the symptoms. There are long-term, sustainable resolutions to control the onset of symptoms of stage fright. For those individuals willing to invest the time, they can have a lifetime of success versus the temporary fix you might find by going straight to your medicine cabinet.

In our anxiety over public speaking, our thoughts instantly go to a scene of us standing at a lectern in front of hundreds of people. Culturally, we are brought up from the time we are young to believe that public speaking and anxiety is synonymous. It would almost seem unnatural if I didn't include the statement that most people fear it more than death. This cultural myth has permeated our thoughts from the beginning, so we often perpetuate the myth by doing everything possible to avoid public-speaking situations. We are inadvertently taught about fearing fear itself.

We often create our own self-fulfilling prophesies. You can run from those presentations in front of hundreds of people periodically. However, each day presents itself with new challenges we could rise above if we simply learned the appropriate techniques to effectively communicate in a public setting, regardless of whether it is with one person or with thousands.

Anxiety is glossed over in a small section of many public-speaking books as being an inevitable part of the equation. Unfortunately, either through genes—which prove that some of us have a higher propensity for that type of anxiety—or cultural inundation of the horrors of public speaking, we all believe we can simply suffer through the few times we'll be required to speak publicly. In some cases, we are pointed toward a quick fix designed to simply get us through a single moment. My goal is to get you to stand tall and confidently present yourself in a commanding and influential manner that will cause the receiver of your message to take notice as a result of the power of your words, gestures, and vocal inflections. I want you to be able to stand in front of a crowd with a smile on your face, and truly mean it. That smile will show the world that you are having fun and that your messages are being heard. I can teach you that the rising heat up the sides of your neck and a flushing face should be an afterthought rather than something that impacts your ability to attain your public speaking goals. In fact, let's strike the afterthought comment, and set a goal to not even think about it at all. With preparation and practice, it is possible.

I have an almost existential view of public speaking. Don't psych yourself up so much that it takes away from your ability to rationally state the points necessary to make an impact, and don't talk yourself down so much that the audience's enthusiasm wanes at your own lack of passion. Repeating the same words, "I can do this, I can do this, I can do this" as you struggle to stand upright on your walk to the lectern most likely won't strengthen your presentation. In addition, the repeated mantra won't resolve your deep-seated fear unless the true investment of practice and preparation are also part of the process. Stage fright may not ever fully go away, but it can be controlled with the right invested actions and efforts. These actions and efforts will most likely all filter back to practice and preparation.

Public speaking is a journey that needs the roller coaster ride for the audience to feel the emotions that you're feeling. The audience wants to be a part of your message and success. They want to walk away with some meaningful, inspirational, or motivational message. Public speaking surrounds us. It is a normal fact in our life and culture. Although technology has changed how we communicate, for the most part we still can't avoid the need to interact in some way on a regular basis. Even if you are more on the latter half of fight or flight when it comes to hitting the topic head on, you will need to use many aspects of public speaking, such as writing or sending a message. Some people would rather communicate behind a computer screen within social media channels, but in this book you will also learn the importance of the written word and understand what your message says about you, the writer. Your personal and professional success is directly linked to your ability to communicate effectively.

3.

Tame the Beast

I just finished a speech for the local Rotary Club. I confidently explained that a few years before, I would have had difficulty presenting to them. Even as a communication major with over twenty years in the corporate world, communicating face-to-face or presenting in front of multiple people created far too many anxious moments in my life that I've repressed from my memory. My experience and background may make some non-believers say that it couldn't have been that bad. I must emphasize that it was *that bad*. I've been demoted twice in my career and was told that I would never reach senior management because I was never seen in the role. Yet, I can confidently tell you that I have never been happier or more satisfied personally or professionally. In the midst of a down-turned economy, I've had more raises, promotions, and increases in job responsibility then I could ever have imagined. I am doing things I never dreamed of, including writing two books and being part of the National Speakers Association (NSA). I give much of the credit to my transformation to my increased confidence level. Learning to get over my stage fright saved my career and created an abundant amount of new opportunities to succeed.

Most people want to improve themselves, including a countless many that have a targeted desire to improve their public-speaking skills. The most difficult part is crossing over the threshold from change-thinking to change-actions. As an example, just look at the countless New Year's resolutions broken immediately after we announce we want to improve ourselves. What I want to provide is a guide to ensure you stay on the right track toward achieving your goals.

Have you ever been lost while driving without having an accessible map or GPS? We have an instant panic attack about what we need to do. The anxiety builds up more with each wrong turn. We lose our ability to think clearly and make rational thoughts. The exact same feeling occurs when we approach the podium to give a speech. Our mind plays tricks on us, which impacts our body. What if you could control if not even *block* these feelings, so you are able to clearly and confidently articulate your points?

I have seen people with normally rampant stage fright who have given amazing eulogies. I found it interesting that these individuals were so caught up in the anguish of death that they forgot, even if for a small moment, that they were supposed to be scared to be in front of a large audience. The thought of the death instantly jumped them to the last stages of what experienced speakers are taught: it's not about you; it's about them, the audience. The frightened thoughts are substituted for ones of passion and love for the deceased. With regular public speaking, you can take actions that will allow you to give rousing speeches and presentations that you once thought were never possible.

In a visual example, here is a picture of my then ten-year-old daughter, right before she was to get her ears pierced:

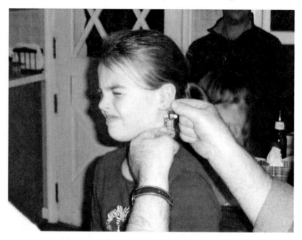

Now, let's see the victorious jubilation of reaching the finish line:

As a general rule of thumb, our minds are often numb to the potential triumph because we are too occupied with the heart-stopping anticipation of what is in front of us. What if you could be trained to think about the endgame and the potential success? It is possible. This book will cover many ways to identify the varying symptoms that often come with the pending act of public speaking. The symptoms are driven by deep-seated causes that we may not even fully understand about ourselves, yet. When you fully recognize the correlation between the onsets of symptoms with the ability to control your thoughts, you will see exponentially greater success, and get a deeper understanding of your own potential.

This practical guide provides examples and techniques that will make it real for you. It will show you that speakers of all levels of experience and anxiety will be capable to retrain their hearts and minds one tip at a time. The ultimate goal is to control the symptoms, and more importantly use them to your advantage to relate to any audience. Here are some examples as to why we get anxious when we think about speaking in public:

- Uncomfortable situation
- New environment
- Potential failure
- Possible embarrassment
- Fear of boring the audience
- Inexperience
- Anticipation buildup

Each of these examples can create the symptoms we fear: dizzy head, heart pounding, shaking, sweating, shallow breathing, and that sick feeling in our stomachs. These symptoms most likely will never go away completely, but they can be controlled with practice and preparation.

In Janet Esposito's book *Getting Over Stage Fright—A New Approach to Resolving Your Fear of Public Speaking and Performing* she discusses approaches that tie in the inclusion of spirituality and meditation to get the mind and body stabilized to find "inner strength for outward support." Her premise is based on the need to understand that the escalation of anxiety is completely normal for most of us. Many actors as they approach the stage have varying levels of fear, but what makes the experienced ones different is their ability to teach themselves to transfer these feelings to their art. The important fact is that there is a direct correlation between your ability to tame the mind and your ability to control the body.

I took a class in college more than twenty years ago on visualization. As I walked into the first class laughing, I was expecting some easy credits. It was taught by one of the university sports coaches, and the class was full of athletes. The study of visualizing and sports psychology was a growing field at the time, and was not fully understood. We were asked to take one routine act, such as shooting foul shots, and start tracking our progress physically as we slowly introduced new mental practices to calm ourselves down. The intent was to visualize our own success and growth through true focus. I was skeptical for much of the semester. I selected a three-mile run that I had been doing for years. I had been doing it for so long that I typically finished close to the same finish time each day. I saw very little room for improvement. There may have been some times when I could sprint through it for a quick event-driven improvement, but the goal of the class exercise was sustained improvement.

I watched in amazement as I worked on my breathing techniques, on measuring my strides, on keeping my arms straight rather than having them come across my chest, and—most importantly—on the belief that I could accomplish more. My times continued to go down regularly. I did reach a plateau, but it was at a stabilized level that was far better than my predicted outcome. Visualizing success is now a common practice among athletes, and it can be important to your own success when preparing for situations that cause stage fright. Maybe the old fictional character, Stuart Smalley, played by Al Franken on Saturday Night Live segment that first aired in 1991, wasn't too far off when he said the following catchphrase into the mirror: "You're good enough, you're smart enough, and doggonit, people like you."

It is now normal to watch athletes and actors visualize their performances. They are making every effort to stretch their peak performance. I recall seeing Olympic skiers on TV with their eyes closed and hands in motion as they simulated their progress through the course. Their hands moved smoothly in unison with their thoughts by going side-to-side and up-and-down to mimic the exact course they were about to go down. I believe that they all saw themselves as the winner.

Limiting thoughts can significantly impact performance. Shaquille O'Neal was a consistently poor free-throw shooter in college and in the NBA. His physical technique was often identified as an issue because of the lack of arc he had when shooting the ball into the hoop. However, as his career continued and more coaches and sports psychologists became involved in his training, his issue was often noted as a mental block. He finished his career with a 52.7-percent success rate. Wikipedia states that in the NBA, most players make between seventy to eighty percent of their attempts. A combination of more mental focus, physical preparation, and practice could have increased these results substantially.

Some people see the deep-rooted causes of their own public speaking as obstacles too large to break through. We fill ourselves with excuses that it's too hard to try to identify and fix due to personal time constraints. We convince ourselves that it's not worth the effort or we are unable to visualize our own success. I was one of those people until I ironically got more personal in a speech and showed a significant amount of vulnerability. I began to sing onstage for part of this speech. My apprehension turned to confidence when I saw the audience's reaction. I was consistently off key and had no rhythm, yet there were tears in the eyes of some of the audience members as they began to relate to the message of my story. You can use your own individual hurdles, roadblocks, and triumphs to strengthen your own message.

There are many options that can be taken to create synergy between your mind, body, and soul. I am not an expert, so I suggest consulting the professionals. However, psychotherapy, hypnotherapy, and yoga have been identified as potential alternatives to prepare you for the big meeting or your moment on stage. I've even turned to the Nintendo Wii game console to do yoga on the Wii Fit Balance Board before some of my speech competitions. The exercises were calming and relaxing, while it focused my attention away from the building tension. I continued this routine before I got mad at the game. It predicts your fitness "age" based on certain physical tests. At the age of 40, it continued to tell me I was over 60 years old. This was not helping my mental stability. I needed to visualize success, not being 20 years older.

Once we understand the potential causes of the fear, we can take the actions to build our confidence level. The psychology of fear can have a devastating direct link to the physical effects of the built-up symptoms. An article from www.owningthestage.com notes that there are certain things you can't control such as "…your genes. Some people are simply more prone to anxiety than others, and if you're unlucky in the DNA you probably know it. Blame your parents. With the genetic factor, you have to play the hand you are dealt." This argument still allows for the possibility that we have the ability to control much of the causes around us. We will cover much of this in detail later in the book. The article does go on to state that:

"It's 'only' in your mind. It's important to understand that stage fright is subjective: it exists only in your mind and your own perception. It might be painful, but it's not like a poke in the eye. It's a purely inner struggle.

Sometimes stage fright can feed on itself, like when you're deathly afraid of getting stage fright! It might seem crazy but we're not talking about rational, logical thoughts here. This leads to a kind of perfect storm of anxiety. You might make a little mistake, like a slightly out of tune note or a badly timed entrance or a loss of balance. That triggers a bit of anxiety, which kicks off your overblown fear of anxiety, which causes a few more mistakes, and so on until you faint, or have a coronary, or at least consider faking one.

And even though stage fright is 'only in your mind,' it is still very real for a lot of people."

The Eric Education Resource Information Center notes that many inadequate theories of stage fright tie into the "cumulative effects of emotions" that include "neurological, body reaction, and a two-factor theory of body reactions and environmental cues." However, they theorize that stage fright goes beyond that to become a culmination of "behavioral, physiological, and the cognitive." In other words, the behaviors of avoiding the situation of public speaking because of perceived failure or embarrassment, leads to physiological symptoms of sweating or shaking that impacts the "consciousness of both." There is a continuum of mind, body, and behavior actions that are related to each other. All can impact our ability to give our best unless they are controlled.

Some ways to prepare for your time in the spotlight include: write out what you want to say; practice by repeating the message often; increase your stage time; and be a student of yourself. Specifically, being a student of yourself can include your ability to be more willing to be open to feedback and videotaping.

As you continue your public speaking growth through mental and physical preparation, you will be taught how to visualize success and how to get to know the audience. Additionally, you will begin to truly *believe* that the audience wants to listen to your message, and understand that not all of your feelings are fear. Some of your built-up anticipation might just be excitement to be there. On the physical front, you can prepare with deep breathing, stretching out the tension, avoiding caffeine, exercising prior to the presentation, and staying within your routine, if possible. Many of these tips will be detailed in later chapters.

You can become a solid public speaker, or simply someone who doesn't faint when they do it. It takes time and effort. However, the preparation and practice are easily accomplished with a commitment to get better, and are not as difficult as you think. The beast of public speaking can be tamed. You can find the way to sustained success. It is time to cross over the threshold from wanting to change to actual change.

4.

Understand that Success is Possible

Here's a phrase I teach often: "It is not bragging if it is a fact." The fact that it took me over twenty years in the workforce to have someone provide, on record (written in my annual performance appraisal), a positive comment about my communication skills gives me the right and obligation to stand on the mountaintop screaming that I now have the skills and confidence to be an effective communicator. You will learn that a person conveying a message does not automatically have the respect and trust of the audience. It must be earned. Part of earning this trust and respect is building credibility with that audience. My intention in this chapter is to build my credibility with you, the audience, by sharing information that will enable you to get to know me and understand who I am as a communicator and leader.

I went to the University of Delaware. On my first day of freshman orientation, I was told I needed to choose a major and "undecided" was not one of the options. My major could change over time, they said, but I had to at least commit to something. I like to say that I picked my major alphabetically. There was no money in Anthropology, so that was out. I never like dissecting a frog, so Biology was not an option. Everyone was in Business, and I wanted to be a little different, so I chose Communication. It didn't hurt that the female-to-male ratio was rumored to be forty to one (the truth was closer to twenty to one, but it didn't seem to help my love life in college, anyway).

Being a painfully shy and introverted individual had the potential to hold me back personally and professionally. I had to take action for myself if I wanted any success in the real world. I was given an early lesson, by being told I had to select a major. I was being forced to take action if I wanted to develop myself. I luckily selected a major that would become a focal point for the rest of my life as I struggled to grasp, improve, and finally sharpen my communication. I am thankful for the choice, even if it still took many more years to gain the confidence to become a master.

My specialty in Interpersonal and Organizational Communication taught me the importance of personal interaction. Both in society and at work, success comes to those who communicate effectively. I had a drive to succeed and saw spurts of success; however, I didn't see the success at the speed I would have wanted. The delayed success was due to my inability to sharpen the skills I had and develop the ones bursting to come out.

I could put two sentences together; in fact, I could put two, three, or eighteen sentences together without a breath. As an introvert, I found that I tried to say everything necessary as quickly as possible in the hope that I would be done as soon as possible. Needless to say, I lacked key communication skills, like knowing the audience or learning to be clear. Having a communication degree did not in itself make me an effective communicator.

After college, my early professional successes were inconsistent. I started on the phones in a collections call center. My shyness was not going away, and I felt it would be better if I didn't have to interact face to face. Except, somewhere, I must have forgotten about the daily interactions with my peers and management. Performance-wise, I achieved decent results and my confidence increased with my ability to speak to customers I didn't have to see. My ability to confidently speak face-to-face to my peers and management team, however, was awkward at best. As long as my numbers spoke for me, I didn't think I needed anything else.

My results did speak for themselves enough to land me a management position, in which I was responsible for leading people who worked on the phones. This was the beginning of a roller coaster ride in success. My inability to effectively connect with people who worked for me and for whom I worked left my confidence shot. I couldn't assertively communicate, let alone give my team the assurance that they were in good hands. Unfortunately, my drive to succeed far outweighed my ability to target specific opportunities. Every time I was knocked down, I worked twice as hard to get back up. I was demoted twice in my corporate life and changed positions often. Sometimes, the frequent positions changes were because I was wanted for my knowledge or skillset, while other times because the company needed to move me on because of my derailing behavior. I was a hard worker, but did not always work smart.

What I didn't realize early on was that I needed a career coach. Objective people were ready to give me advice, but I was not proactive enough to ask for it and I was too defensive to accept it. My introverted behavior did not let enough people get to know the true me. They saw only the surface me. I was a hard driven, dedicated individual who had trouble sending and receiving messages. My overall success was stagnating and possibly moving in the wrong direction.

From Fear to Success

I have now worked at one of the largest financial institutions in the United States, Bank of America (previously MBNA), for over twenty years. I have been in a variety of roles, ranging from people management to administration, and just about everything else in between. Within the last six years, my company was bought, faced the global recession, and made an announcement of significant future job cuts. Considering how internally focused I was, it took me far too long to realize that I had to be my own career coach. I learned that career effectiveness and professional development came through a proactive approach and a desire to improve. With the potential ramifications of the macroeconomics swirling around me, I started to realize that I had no choice. I needed help.

Once the choice was made to take a more proactive approach to improve myself, I significantly improved my ability to communicate up, to communicate down, and to communicate to peers and business partners. Confidence was gained in my ability to network, with that self-confidence bubbling over in my presentation skills. I was beginning to take an active leadership approach, which in turn made a difference in the businesses I oversaw and interacted with.

Action had to be taken so I was not left behind. I didn't want to hide and hope when key employment decisions were made. I wanted to do more than survive; I wanted to thrive. My communication skills were my Achilles heel, and I needed to fix them. You may not believe the extent of my opportunities, so I thought I would share some examples of communication-specific quotes directly from more than twenty years of my performance appraisals:

"Tom needs to be more concise with his communication style. He needs to ensure he understands his audience and his ability to adapt based on who he is interacting with."

"[Tom needs to] ask questions to ensure a full understanding."

"Position ideas with your audience in mind…need to be more confident in presentations to senior management; don't second guess-self."

"Avoid shutting down when others don't agree with you."

There were far too many years of running on a treadmill of feedback without jumping at my main opportunities: communication, leadership, and confidence. These are the skills needed most in the business world! Maybe my problem was that I didn't always believe the feedback; as a communication major, I believed the skills were already there. Maybe the skills were simply being overlooked somehow or not accurately being assessed.

It finally began to sink in that I would never advance—or that my job might actually be on the line—if I didn't take steps to improve. I still took the slow train to improvement; but at least I got onboard. The theme: I had to finally cross a threshold and break myself out of my comfort zone; I needed to get past my trepidation. Baby steps were taken toward the process of improvement, but at least I was moving in the right direction. Even with a slow process, there was momentum. Once I saw my actions begin to generate praise and increased responsibility, I went on a mission to proactively grasp the most effective ways to improve my communication and leadership skills. Although no two paths are the same for any individual, I thought I would share the actions taken that made a difference in my career.

• I found some trusted mentors.

• I became a mentor (shockingly, teaching others reinforced what I needed myself).

• I started a networking routine to meet with senior leaders I didn't know.

- I gained courage and forced myself to ask key development questions in one-on-one settings and group settings. I began asking anyone and everyone, "What can I do to improve?" After some hesitation and surprise at the question, people were more than willing to share their thoughts and appreciated that I was asking. It seemed as if my mistakes were almost a side note to the main discussion, since people knew I was giving the maximum effort to make myself stronger.
- When feedback was provided, I always followed-up with, "How?" If someone tells you to be faster, more efficient, more effective, etc., you are still not being given the direction needed to improve. You have to ask, "How?"
- I joined Toastmasters.
- I stopped worrying about what people thought of me and started paying more attention to just getting the job done. I put effort into developing the skills needed to gain trust and respect for the work I was doing (the rest would take care of itself).
- After more than twenty years, I finally saw in writing the following comment: "Tom's organizational and communication skills are his key strengths."

This was the first time I didn't read that I needed to improve something in my communication. The biggest change was my confidence. I was also learning the importance of two-way dialogue. Although still introverted, I was beginning to understand the power of building strong relationships, a skill that needs to always be honed and will always work for you.

I want to share a story of how a little action can turn into a big success. After joining Toastmasters, I began working through the various certifications in communication and leadership. My managers at work became aware of the certifications and started to recognize me. The word slowly spread to groups of people who didn't know me. When they did get to know me, it was as "an effective communicator." My past communication gaps were being left behind. In social settings where I had previously kept quiet, I now threw in a couple of conversation starters about my public-speaking endeavors. These conversations led to strong friendships and beneficial networking. I was even getting invitations outside my company to speak to other organizations.

Word continued to spread within my corporate environment. I was tapped on the shoulder at a meeting of local managers and my peer asked me to meet with her newer managers about effective communication. It was hard to imagine! The person told far too many times that he needed to improve his communication skills was being asked to teach others how to communicate. I was in heaven. People started to listen to me. They actually sought my advice and messages because I could confidently convey them in a way that was easily understood and relate to them to the audience. I shared my mistakes and showed them that they, too, could persevere and succeed. I was gaining credibility from a group of people who saw my own growth and through that recognized that they, too, could improve.

My informal professional-development series was getting attention. Another manager in a different department asked if I could formalize the event and speak to his group of managers monthly. These sessions were a hit, and they morphed into topics that people could pragmatically develop and use for their own individual development: writing résumés, networking, organizing, managing time, managing different generations, interviewing, and, of course, overcoming fear of public speaking. The series then made me eligible for the National Speakers Association (NSA).

A month after getting into the NSA, I was selected as the 2010-11 District 45 Toastmaster of the Year. I was pleasantly surprised and humbled to see that my work was starting to pay off not just for myself, but for others. It was an honor to be selected to represent my district, knowing that there are only eighty-one Toastmaster Districts in the world (representing over 270,000 members). I felt like I was living the book *If You Give a Mouse a Cookie*. As the author Laura Joffe Numeroff writes, "If you give a mouse a cookie, he's going to ask for some milk. When you give him some milk, he'll probably ask you for a straw." The story continues with constant add-ons. In my case, I was finding ways to succeed that fed the motivation to want more. This painfully shy and introverted individual was making a name for himself in the field of public speaking.

As a teacher and mentor, not only was I improving other people's careers, I was improving my own, because I had to practice what I preached. More importantly, I was managing my time effectively, building a strong network, and constantly finding ways to improve. I was making a difference to others and making myself stronger. All of this happened because I finally took action to improve my communication skills and gain confidence in my abilities—something that required more than just a simple leap of faith.

In order to set myself on this road initially, I knew I needed to take action to increase my confidence. I knew I needed Toastmasters. I even lied to myself that the only reason I was joining was to kick-start a dormant corporate club on my company campus that had not met in over a year. My original thoughts were simply to build up my résumé.

I had no idea how it would change my life after I joined in September 2008. The people I have met over the years through that organization provided encouragement and support to participate in speech contests. I moved from an unofficial club consultant to the Vice President of Education. Our club, Dirigo ("I Lead") Toastmasters, went from not holding a meeting in over a year to being well respected within District 45, which includes over one hundred clubs within Maine, New Hampshire, Vermont, and the Canadian provinces of Prince Edward Island, New Brunswick, and Nova Scotia. I now hold advanced communication and advanced leadership certifications with the organization, including a High Performance Leadership (HPL) certification for writing my first book based on the professional development series. My successes seemed to be never ending, simply because I stared my fears in the face and won.

The contests have always tested my will to break down the constant trepidation and angst of being in front of a large group of people. I may never get rid of these feelings entirely, but the shakes, sweats, and heat rushing up from my neck to my ears are no longer the first and only feelings I get. I am now full of energy and excitement to share my messages and stories with the audience.

I found consistent success when competing in speech contests, which only pushed me to go further. I have entered all types of contests to broaden my skill set and to continue to test my comfort zone specific to humorous speeches, inspirational speeches, impromptu speeches, and speech evaluations. I have been fortunate enough to represent the state of Maine on multiple occasions in these contests.

I may need to change the word "consistent." Actually, I have found inconsistency as the pressure has tightened at the higher levels. I have forgotten words in competition, frozen on stage because I could not remember the first line of my speech, and even repeated lines when I had a shot at advancing to the Toastmasters International World Semifinals. I have presented with an actual jackhammer behind me and watched in horror as props were knocked over. I wouldn't want it any other way.

A speech will never be perfect and I was learning to keep moving forward after I made mistakes. More importantly, I had to identify the next actions needed for me to improve the next time. I was growing as a speaker when I actively sought to be better. I took on a mentor after my first taste of the bigger stage when I went to the Toastmasters District 45 International Finals in May 2009, one who has reached the World Semi-finals three times (and advanced to the World Finals once). His advice as a formal mentor and fellow competitor forced me to develop. I have even changed my practice routines: where I previously ensured that the house was dead quiet before practicing, I now can't wait for my kids' piano rehearsals to start. I also invite the howling dog into the room so I have distractions while I refine my skills. The goal is to strive for perfection and grow from the experience. No speech experience will ever be the same, but we should always strive to make it the best it can be.

The premise of this book is not to turn every reader into a professional speaker. The business of professional speaking is an art that needs constant nurturing. However, simple effective communication needs the same cultivation. Everyday skills that can be practiced and refined will turn an ordinary interaction into an extraordinary experience. Your enjoyment and success will skyrocket, along with your confidence level. I am not on the road each day pounding the pavement looking for speaking gigs. I have a day job. However, after years of toiling with being average and inconsistent, I have taken actions needed to succeed.

I'm not the most charismatic person. However, I am now building a strong name for myself because I am learning to relate to people with a message they want to hear. More importantly, I am proud of my ability to finally do something that needed to be done years before. My simple message will resonate with any audience at the core of their thoughts and beliefs.

1. Effective public speaking is more about confidence than communication skills.
2. Public speaking is more than a lectern, podium, or microphone; it is everywhere.
3. The ability to speak publicly is not as hard as you may imagine— the hardest part is taking the first steps.
4. Public speaking is a learned skill that must continually be developed.
5. Your own success, both personal and professional, is correlated to your ability to communicate effectively.

As an audience member listening to presentations for years, I feel qualified to recognize what people want to hear. You should, too. As a public speaker, I have always had a clear vision for what I wanted, but often avoided the situation or taking the actions necessary to improve. I have found confidence and success on the other side of the podium. I know that I now have the skills and self-belief necessary to provide what the audience wants and needs. You too have a strong message inside you right now that is ready to come out. If I can make a difference by transforming my fear into success, you can, too.

PART II

Road to Success

The Anxiety

5.

Identify Why You're Anxious

Many of us tend to stay in our comfort zones. When we wander out of these comfort zones, we start to feel anxious. New situations always increase the stress meter. As previously noted, driving in an unfamiliar place without a map or GPS creates that same feeling that washes over us when we step up to a podium or have that big meeting with the boss. The feeling is natural. There are plenty of actors and athletes who get this same feeling before a big event. It is natural. Given an opportunity to present to senior executives at my company, I instantly fear failing in front of them. They trust and have faith that this presentation will be successful, and I never want to let them down. The mental head games we play with ourselves tell us that the risk of failure is there. However, we need to override this feeling by looking at the other side of the coin: that success is likely if we have controlled everything we could and have come prepared. The presentation won't be perfect, so get over it—you can still make it a great performance if you invest the time and effort.

The punishing effects of the mental game can overtake you. *What if I embarrass myself? What if the red blotches creep up my neck to my face and I am burning with heat?* What if the fear of the fear is overtaking me? *What if…what if…what if?* A funny thing happened as I learned how to practice and prepare. The more stage time I got, the more confident I became. I had worried about the "blush" factor for too many years, and now the only time I ever think about it is when I am teaching people about how I forgot about it. It truly is no longer a distracting "what if" thought. You too can control the mental game by increasing your time on stage.

You also don't want to bore the audience. You won't, as long as you put the necessary time and effort into the material, message, and delivery to ensure you keep the audience interested. Don't just throw the presentation together and hope it works. You have to remember that most people in an audience want you to succeed, and when you succeed, they walk away thinking about you and your message. If your goal is to entertain, inspire, motivate, or persuade, and they are entertained, inspired, motivated, or persuaded, you have both won. Audiences want to think and be transformed into your world. Take the bold and confident approach. When you believe that you have the message to make a difference in someone's life, that belief should turn into confidence that will resonate with any audience. Turn your words to action, and your action into positive energy. If you say, "I'm really glad to be here," you should mean it. *You* set the tone.

Finally, a lack of public-speaking experience often drives anxiety. Nothing increases experience more than just doing more of it. So it's time to set up a plan to increase your face time, presentation time, and public time to gain this experience. As you will learn later in the book, when you start to write and prepare for the audience and stop worrying about yourself, many of these anxious feelings will dissipate.

6.

Know Symptoms Are Coming

While teaching public speaking, I have scared a few people when I've asked, "Who is ready to give a two-minute presentation on [pick a topic]?" Instantly, the stomach sinks, the palms sweat, and the body tremors start. I myself have always battled a red face and blotchy skin; you can tack on tense shoulders and an instant upright stance for me, as well. I've had them all. What was harder than the experience was getting past the fact that the physical reaction was normal. When you are suddenly called on in a business meeting or invited to speak unexpectedly, you probably have a pretty good idea what will happen to you individually. No two people will react the same way, so know *your own* potential reaction so that you can mentally and physically prepare. I will provide more detailed information on mental and physical preparation in upcoming chapters, but the main point in this section is to understand the power of knowing what's coming. Being conscious of it is half the battle. Your ability to anticipate what's next will put you in a different state of mind, and, therefore, your reaction to what lies ahead will be more settled and stable.

7.

Recognize It May Never Go Away

No. The anxiety never completely goes away for most speakers. Before you stop reading, understand that the anxious symptoms can simply become a re-focused energy source for you. We've all heard the so-called fact that people would rather die than speak publicly. I've known speakers who sweat, and we have all felt our own heart pounding at what feels like a million beats per second. It happens. The challenge is being able to control these reactions enough that they can actually help us to become better speakers. Much of my own anxiety was less fear and more buildup of energy bursting to come out. I have found that I can use this energy within my presentation to engage the audience and channel it into my stage presence.

The butterflies in my stomach may be fluttering, and my legs may be shaking, but I also know ahead of time that they're coming. Can I redirect them to help me stride onto the stage with purpose, or integrate stronger physical aspects of my speech and thus use the energy to my advantage? Try to understand the most prevalent symptoms you typically get and diagnose what alternate actions you can take to strengthen your message and delivery. Knowing that the feeling may never completely go away can work to your advantage once you stop fighting it and start working to control it, and then use it to enhance your performance.

8.

Control and Prepare

So, if the anxiety never fully goes away but can be controlled, how do we get there? Control comes with practice and preparation. Try to imagine me at my first state-level speech contest when I couldn't remember the first line, but I could remember the second line. The couple seconds' gaffe felt like it lasted a couple of hours. Then, imagine the moment when I had my shot to go to the World Championship Semi-finals, and I repeated a line two minutes into the presentation. In both cases, I actually gave two of the best speeches of my life, after the mistakes, because I knew I had lost the competition and just wanted to do the rest to prove to myself and the audience that I had a good reason to be there.

I had to change my preparation routine. I couldn't just recite the lines in my car to myself any longer. I had to work on the presentation itself, including my gestures, my stage location, and my pauses. I needed to get out in front of more people. I attempted to contact every Rotary Club, Kiwanis Club, and Lions Club within a thirty-mile radius. I put videos on YouTube and asked for advanced feedback from well-established speakers. I involved my family more; in fact, I have received some of the most critical and useful feedback from my eleven-year-old, thirteen-year-old, and fifteen-year-old children once

I asked them to become an active part of the process.

What I found with better preparation and practice was how to be myself. Before, I'd been trying to become an actor, or act like one of my role models. My enhanced preparation techniques and routines taught me to be me. I also found the best way to mitigate the anxiety was to practice as if it was the real presentation every time. This better practice technique was making me more comfortable in my own skin. Personally, I needed to make the speaking process natural. Counter-intuitively, practicing more intensely actually did make me more relaxed and improved my ability to be who I wanted to be on stage.

The following represent key factors to consider within your preparation regimen: (many of which will be explained in detail later).

• Write it out in full, or at least an outline to cover key thoughts

• Either memorize the whole speech or cut down to note cards, but don't wing it

• When practicing, go through the entire presentation; even when you make mistakes, don't stop

• Choose your words carefully, taking into consideration the order, the rhythm, and the intended impact

• Clearly mark the points to emphasize and/or repeat; write out your cues

• Practice in front of a mirror, friends, family, and colleagues

• Carefully add impactful physical aspects to the speech (e.g., facial expressions, gestures)

• Increase your presentation practice time and stage time; commit to it and speak frequently

• Get familiar with the setting

• Control what you can control (e.g., lighting, temperature, amplification, table/chair set-up)

• Be a student of yourself: videotape yourself, be open to feedback, play to your strengths, minimize self-caused distractions (e.g., paper shuffling, filler words)

• Use familiar experiences: who knows you better than yourself? Talk about what you know; share your stories.

9.

Practice Mental Preparation

Can you visualize your own success? Do you believe—I mean truly believe—that the audience wants to hear your message? If there are people in the audience, than the answer to that question is yes. You must believe the audience is there for you. They want you to succeed or they wouldn't be there. Dale Carnegie once said, "You can conquer almost any fear if you will only make up your mind to do so. For remember, fear doesn't exist anywhere except in the mind." Have you ever seen world-class athletes close their eyes and run through their performance in their minds? As mentioned in the "Tame the Beast" section of this book, if you've ever watched the Winter Olympics, you may remember camera shots of the skiers visualizing the course. You can see their head, body, and hands in the appropriate position as if they were actually on the slopes already. You can do the same thing with a speech.

My wise wife once told me to never ask a question you don't want the answer to, such as, "Do you think that woman is pretty?" In one of my first district-level Toastmasters competitions, I must have been thinking of the early Olympics, where only amateurs competed. I overheard a couple of conversations and was surprised to hear that some of the competitors were professional speakers. I began to ask them about it while we were milling about before the big contest. I instantly convinced myself that I couldn't compete at this level against these professional speakers. I was done before I started because I didn't believe in my own success.

Additional mental preparation includes knowing who your audience is and who you are talking to. Are they a supportive Toastmasters' audience where it is ingrained to applaud loudly? Have you done your due diligence to have a better idea of what you are walking into? Knowing who the audience is and what they may expect should help in your preparation, thus easing your fear and anxiety. The unknown is what often causes much of the angst. Reduce the unknown and you will build up your confidence level.

Finally, there is no right or wrong way to mentally prepare. As much as the many so-called experts opine about preferred styles and personalities, there are multiple ways to get our mental faculties ready for the big presentation. The fact that you are willing (although your mind may be saying otherwise) should tell you that you are well on your way. You may even find that once you pass the threshold of your peak fear, you actually *enjoy* your time in front of the audience.

10.

Question if Fear is Really Fear

Understanding the nature of fear is extremely helpful in getting past it. I am not a clinical expert who can diagnose fear's exact root causes, but I can identify and relate with being outside my comfort zone. Anytime we are in a new situation, we may feel anxiety, fear, stress, discomfort, or whatever you want to call it. What are we afraid of? We may fear failure or embarrassment (*will I be boring?*). Do you fear this may lead to a poor performance? Is this driving you toward your own self-fulfilling prophecy? What if you turned fear around and recognized that it may actually be the rush of anticipation, energy, and excitement waiting to break out? Maybe deep down inside you can't wait to be out there to have your moment with the audience. You may not feel this at first, but over time, you will understand that fear is similar to many positive feelings. When you are waiting in line for the big roller coaster, you get the same butterflies. It is an adrenaline rush that may be more about anticipation than actual fear of the ride. Could it be that your fear of public speaking induces those same feelings of excitement? Fear can be transformed—especially since it may not be fear at all. Maybe you're simply feeling impatience and anticipation about sharing your message.

11.

Practice Physical Preparation

What do you do when the anxiety and panic have moved from a mental to a physical problem? You begin by playing mind games with yourself, and all of a sudden your heart is beating out of control, your hands are sweating, and your stomach is about to double over with the worry of being in the public eye. You must understand that you do have some control. Notice I wrote "some" and not "total." As stated earlier, we need to accept the fact that the anxiety may never go away completely. However, can you use the built-up energy to your advantage? Let's start with the easiest step—take deep breaths. I mean really deep. Not quick and shallow to say you did it, but deep down to your diaphragm. Next, find where the tension is building up. Is it in your neck, shoulders, or fingers? Like an athlete, begin to ease the tension by stretching out the parts of your body that need it most. By concentrating on relaxing the tension in specific sections of your body, you will ease the mental games and feel the physical tension dissipate.

Additionally, you should prepare ahead of time to minimize the physical symptoms for the presentation. This can be accomplished by getting plenty of rest and by avoiding caffeine. I found myself in front of over one hundred individuals at a presentation at the local YMCA when my hands and arms began to shake uncontrollably. Interestingly,

I felt great that day and did not feel nervous at all. I realized I'd had a soda with caffeine in it a couple of hours before the event. Although I was not nervous, I was excited and found that when the building adrenaline kicked in, the caffeine decided to join in the fun.

Another way to stay limber and control your body is through exercise. In addition to having a normal cardiovascular routine that keeps your heart strong, you should try to exercise a couple of hours prior to the presentation, if possible, to get the blood flowing and your body stabilized. Some people like to use meditation and yoga as other means to prepare themselves. The final tip is to stay within as much of your own routine as possible. The routine adds further stability, due to your familiarity with what's going on around you. This mental comfort will add to your physical comfort.

12.

Stop Telling Me to Relax— It Only Makes Me Tense

Nothing brings on tension more than someone telling you to relax. Before some important presentations, I remember good-intentioned people telling me to relax. I often would put my arms to my side and would instantly straighten up as my way to relax. I became as stiff as a board as soon as the word "relax" was used. I obviously wasn't intentionally attempting to look tense in my efforts to relax, but nothing seemed to work as my shoulders stiffened.

If telling me to relax won't work, then what does? Speak frequently. Those who haven't made the determined leap yet to improve their public-speaking skills may do the opposite by avoiding every situation possible. I know, because I was one of them. The more I avoided the situations, the more intense the elevated anxiety would be prior to the inevitable time when I did have to finally speak publicly. I learned that I had to speak, and speak, and speak some more. I began to volunteer to present. Volunteers are often asked for, and, obviously, not everyone jumps at these requests. I also became proactive in contacting friends, family, and colleagues and asking to practice a speech in front of them. I have started many emails with, "I have an odd request…," asking to practice in front of a group at work who had nothing to do with the topic I was talking about. I have found very few times when people have said no. My goal is to get to a point at which I look so relaxed that people don't need to tell me to relax.

13.

Play to Your Strengths

What makes you happy? Which subjects are you a master of? I am not the greatest humorist storyteller around. Although I am improving, humorous storytelling is not my strength. I have plenty of funny stories, but my delivery and passion are better geared toward inspirational and motivational messaging. I can sprinkle humorous anecdotes throughout a presentation to emphasize points, but I stick to my strengths. You should continue to work on your own aspects that need improving, but keep to what makes you special. The differentiating factors should be a focal point of your speeches. If you are a high-energy speaker, get out from behind the lectern and use the stage to your advantage. Your strengths are a direct reflection of your confidence level and as you play more to these strengths the chances are much greater that you will deliver a stellar performance.

14.

Do Something with
Your Hands and Arms

Oh, those pesky hands and arms! Unless the speaker has some natural or rehearsed specific movements, many speakers' hands and arms have been known to:

- flail around
- hide in pockets
- perch on hips
- hide behind backs
- clench into fists

This chapter is intentionally placed under the "Anxiety" category because nothing screams nerves more than people uncomfortable with their arms and hands. As formal as it may appear at first, always have your arms at your side unless they are in the middle of intentional actions or come up as a natural movement. The hands should also be unclenched; a clenched fist is a visible indicator of your anxiety. I was once given the advice that if nerves start to creep in, to rub your thumb against your palm in each hand; the subtle act of your thumb rubbing your palm allows your hands to remain at your side and still appears normal. Over time, you will become naturally looser. Additionally, hands touching—either fingers together or fingertips touching—or hands behind your back often give the audience an uptight feeling, especially if it is prior to you starting your presentation. Having your arms at your side should be like home base—your default position before your next gesture. This position took a little getting used to when I first started, since I tensed up my shoulders with the straight arms, but over time it truly becomes a comfortable launching point for your hands.

15.

Don't Let Personality be an Excuse

I'*m too shy, too introverted, too loud, too boisterous, too extroverted, too technical, too judgmental, or too energetic to be a decent public speaker.* The list can go on and on as to why people lack the confidence to speak publicly. Many other reasons seem to revolve around being too quiet and withdrawn; however, it doesn't mean that you don't have a message to send. Conversely, attention-grabbing extroverts have told me that they fear being in front of a group of people because of the risk of blurting out something ill-advised or untimely.

No two public speakers are exactly alike. Public speaking needs all types of personalities in order to relate to the many diverse audience's expectations. However, this is not just about the business of public speaking; it's about the personal side. You can use your own personality and interests as strong tools. If you are a "sports junky," find ways to include that in your presentations. It is important, however, to make sure you are being thoughtful and inclusive when talking about your own personal topics, such as sports and adventures that make you happy and comfortable. When using sports metaphors, for example, you should ensure that audiences will understand your references. I would avoid an American football metaphor like "Monday morning quarterback" if I was speaking in the United Kingdom, for example, since the popularity of the sport is not necessarily widespread there. As long as you are certain you and your audiences are on the same page, you can recount personal experiences playing or even watching events. You can describe how you felt when pushed to the limits or lessons you learned after a loss.

I like to share a story about when the 2004 Boston Red Sox were losing the American League Championship to the New York Yankees three games to zero in the seven-game series. I was invited by a friend who was a Yankees fan to go to game four at Fenway Park in Boston. No Major League Baseball (MLB) team had ever come back to win a series after losing the first three games. The Red Sox made a dramatic comeback in the ninth inning to tie the game. They won it in spectacular fashion with a homerun to win the game in the bottom of the twelfth inning. The Red Sox eventually became the first MLB team to ever win a series like this. The story and its messages have so many different twists and turns that can be tailored to many different audiences' tastes and expectations. I typically share that my Yankees friend conveniently needed to leave with the game tied at the top of the twelfth inning. In one of the arguably greatest baseball games ever played, I simply say that I heard the cheering outside the stadium since I was walking to the car. I never saw it. The message, which I temper with humor in the story, is: never walk away from potentially historic moments.

You can try infusing your personality and interests into a presentation to play to your strengths, if you can ensure that there are messages and points that relate back to the audience. This allows you to control the content that is meaningful to you and allows your own personality to shine because it has significance to you. You can also test and share your personality with others. Maybe you start with a more intimate audience sitting around a conference table. I often felt when I was first beginning that one of my strengths was one-on-one conversational teaching, and the smaller audience gave me the base to build my confidence and public-speaking skills. I began to expand my messaging to a few people around a table before taking it to a class of fifteen to twenty people. The process expanded as my strengths grew with my confidence. Your personality is who you are, but it should never be used as an excuse to avoid the opportunity to make you stronger. You can use your personality to your advantage, while also pushing further to transform over time into the person you want to be. No two speakers are exactly alike, and that is a good thing. Regardless of the personality you have shaped for yourself, you can grow into a successful public speaker.

16.

Stop Comparing Yourself to Great Orators

I *can't speak like that!* You see someone on TV or go to a presentation and see someone who can speak circles around you. You might say *I will never be like him or her, so why try?* And so, our fear increases and our confidence falters because we have set the wrong bar. The bar is you. It may be nice to aspire to be someone whom you admire and want to emulate. The goal should be to reach the level of the *better* speakers, but the comparison should be how much you have improved yourself. If you said "um" and "ah" thirty-seven times in a five-minute speech, then your goal should be something less than thirty-seven the next time around. If you put others on a pedestal, you may never get on it. Set small improvement increments and aspire to attain them. Once they are reached, set more goals. Keep raising your own bar. You may be surprised at your own ascent.

17.

Be Different—Be You

We see a speaker we enjoy, and we often want to be like him or her. Instead of emulating that person, however, try taking some of the things you like about the speaker and adding them to your repertoire. Some great things about great speakers should be copied: some speakers use vocal variety well, others have strong stage presence, and still others can tell a story simply with their hand gestures and facial expressions. You should, however, find what makes you who you are and strengthen that. *Your* success will be based on your ability to connect with an audience and have them take away your messages. Audiences should remember you for *your* signature style, not because you speak like (insert name here). While you grow as a speaker, find what has worked for you and keep refining it. Your niche is there; it just needs to be nourished. I watched plenty of videos of Toastmasters World Champions of Public Speaking and other successful presenters, but it was when I began to simply watch, listen, and enjoy the speeches rather than trying to copy them that I truly felt like I was making progress in achieving my goals.

18.

It's Alright to Have a "Stage" Me — It's Still Me

It almost seems contradictory to have a section about finding your personal niche immediately followed by how different you may appear on stage. Let me explain. My wife watched some of my speeches and videos in disbelief and commented how different I was on stage. I was different on stage, to some extent, for many reasons. My confidence level had been rising, and I was developing an emerging personality comfortable enough at a podium to send strong messages. All of this is much different from sitting around the dinner table chatting. The stage me is still the "real" me; I am not being an actor up on stage. I couldn't be acting and still genuinely believe that my message would effectively relate and connect with the audience.

As my confidence continued to soar, I began to reconnect the stage me with the off-stage me. I'm sure I've narrowed the gap a little, but there will still most likely be differences. The important point is that it is still me up there. If you remember, I am typically introverted naturally, so I had to work hard on my stage presence to ensure I had the right impact. When I first videotaped myself, I had to ask, "Is that really me?" The answer was always yes. When I received feedback that I looked different on stage or on camera, I was all right with that. It is always fun trying different material and in some cases pushing the limits of my personality, to meet audience needs. You need to be comfortable knowing that there may be a different stage you, and feel good about the fact that that can still be the real you.

19.

Listen to Yourself After You're Done Listening to Everyone Else

Besides listening to your heart pitter-patter out of control, you should absorb all of the feedback provided to you. You will get feedback from multiple sources. Be a sponge and take it all in. It's important to maintain a thick skin and truly think about the feedback provided, to determine how it can most enhance your presentation. Once you've adequately taken it all in, you should then decide if it is right for you. We all become better when we get help. We should thirst for feedback.

It's important to understand, however, that you are not required to adopt all of it. You can find a middle ground. The balanced approach says that you appreciate and respect the feedback, but you are ultimately the final decision maker in what you choose to present and how you present it. This fact alone should give you the comfort and confidence that you are presenting a work that you will be proud of, and that you believe in your message. It is *your* message. If someone's suggestions ever cause any deviation from this, you should determine whether or not you really want to take that feedback. It is not easy saying no to someone who presented you with the gift of feedback, but you must remember that you are the one standing at the podium.

20.

Use Fear as a Motivator

If anticipation of speaking publicly still puts knots in your stomach, then use it as motivation. Fear does different things to different individuals. Some people become paralyzed and simply choose to do nothing. Yes, nothing is an option—but there are better options. Avoiding having to present in front of a large group is possible. However, conversations with a client you are trying to sell to or negotiating with individuals will happen in your day-to-day business. Even normal personal interactions may require assertive and confident communication that will only generate fear because you have convinced yourself through the infamous avoidance technique that you are not ready. Avoidance, as a solution, is probably not your best course of action to get over the fear.

Fear can become a motivator that can push you harder, make you more creative, and get you to dig deeper. It can drive you to do your due diligence to prepare for the unexpected or avoid making similar mistakes going forward. You can hit things head on that are the root causes of your fear. Personally, I had to take a different tack in my own preparation after I forgot certain sections of an important speech. I immediately changed when, where, and how often I practiced. Additionally, now when I start to feel anticipation and angst building up, I find extra time to pull out the material again and make sure I know it inside and out.

You do have some control. If you are afraid your message won't stick, invest a significant amount of time into the content and delivery, to *make sure* the message will stick. If you are uncomfortable with your knowledge of the material, study it and become a subject-matter expert. If you are afraid you are too inexperienced, find stage time to get more experience. Even with all of this, you should understand that despite putting in preparation time and doing your homework, mistakes will be made—no matter how hard you work. You must simply commit to learning from them. Don't let this thing called fear hold you back; see it as the guiding force to get you where you want to be. Stare it in the face, and suddenly your motivation will move you further toward your personal and professional goals. Remember that this natural feeling is holding many others back; by taking actions to reduce the impact fear has on you, you have differentiated yourself from many others. That, in itself, is success.

Make Your Message Count

21.

Have a Different Set of Eyes on It

Whether you are working on the first or the fifteenth draft of a speech, always seek advice from a friend, a family member, or anyone available throughout the process. It is sound advice to use friends and family to help improve speech delivery. It is also important to get them involved even earlier in the process by looking at the written content. If possible, try to have someone similar to the intended audience (who may more easily relate to the message) see if he or she can grasp the points you are attempting to make. That may not always be possible, but don't trust that you have nailed down your content until others have read it. I have seen myself and others wait too long before having friends and family take a look. This actually creates more work, since you have most likely started memorizing the speech and you may now have to go back and recreate new portions. Find someone with an objective point of view to read through it first.

There may not always be a major overhaul, but changing a single word or re-ordering a sentence can change the audience reaction from a "that's nice" reaction to "Wow!" I once finished in third place in a speech contest. There were only three people in the contest. The feedback I received revolved around the audience not fully understanding my message because the key point wasn't revealed until the end. By simply moving the message to the front and re-emphasizing the point later, I saw tears of joy shed because of my newly *revised* inspirational message. My speech today would have been collecting dust as a one-time message if I hadn't invested time finding people to read through it in detail.

22.

Make Outlines a Powerful Tool

We finally select a topic and get over our writer's block. We begin to write out our speech start to finish. Even if we convince ourselves that we will re-work it and refine it, we have left the speech structure potentially in shambles. The process is backwards if we write it, then go back and check to ensure that we have an effective opening, body, and conclusion. We should start with the seed of an idea. The seed may even come out of our folder or notebook of random speech ideas and topics that we want to germinate.

The idea should have the speech intent, message, and audience take-away applied before we add any other text. We need to ensure that the message is clear and the intended effects (e.g., inspiration, motivation, persuasion) are laid out. Before you even begin the writing process, the formulation of a clear message starts with an answer to the question: "What's the purpose of your presentation, speech, or project?" If you can't answer this question, how can you expect your audience to get it? Once the purpose is clear and you have clearly defined your thesis, you are ready to continue massaging the message. Once the message is readily seen, you can then outline the most effective ways to open and close. You can apply the points you want to support the message, and then include memorable stories that speak to these points.

Effective public speaking starts with a strong foundation. The outline is that foundation, on which everything else is built.

23.

Write Out Your Speech

I have heard too many people say that they work well under pressure. I have also heard people say that they are subject-matter experts or have done a presentation so many times that they can just "wing it." My only response is, "Good luck." You will find that effective public speakers are constantly preparing. That preparation is crucial to ensuring that your audience gets the key points you want them to walk away with. If you "wing it," you are potentially leaving out critical points. Your ability to be clear and concise and to stay on track will also be jeopardized.

Writing out the speech in its entirety as the next step after writing an outline ensures that you have a clear plan of attack for covering everything you want covered. Additionally, writing out the speech ensures that you have a full arsenal of economical words for your audience to absorb. A message hits home more quickly and more effectively when you are succinct and thoughtful. You can take the fully scripted speech, after you have practiced it successfully, and trim it back down to an outline or key points you want to make. You should know the script well enough by then that the appropriate points will be emphasized and not forgotten.

Isn't the ability to think quickly on your feet without a script important to your success? I would answer "yes," with a caveat. Impromptu speaking skills are crucial to your growth as a speaker; they help you handle the question-and-answer part, deal with tough audiences, and adapt your material based on the audience's reaction. However, impromptu speaking is really just an extension of well-prepared speaking. The speaker still needs to keep the speech on point and within the expected time limit. The success I have seen with people speaking off the cuff has been sporadic, at best, and rarely duplicated consistently.

24.

Write Your Own Introduction

Avoid surprises by knowing exactly what is being said about you in your introduction prior to getting up to speak to any audience. The unknown can add to your angst and leave some risks out there for you to then deal with when you come up next. For example, if you are familiar with the introducer, he or she may share anecdotes that duplicate your prepared material. Additionally, the information may not be factually correct if the master of ceremonies did not check with you first. Introductions set the tone for the entire presentation and must be strong to allow for a smooth and effective transition to the featured speaker.

Imagine having a boring or a surprising introduction before you get on. Your shocked face as you approach the lectern or your need to scramble to transition to get back on track may be awkward. In addition to ensuring that your introduction is the way you want it written, you should also invest time with the person introducing you to go over your expectations. You will want to ensure that he or she emphasizes key points you want stressed. Early on, I handed my introduction to my presenters with minimal preparation. It didn't take long to see how many introducers tended to wing it, read my prepared introduction incorrectly, or skip over key facts. At times, I found I needed to invest valuable energy recovering my introduction. The introduction should be considered, and written as, a short speech. As a speaker, you should control factors around you, and the introductory speech is one of them.

25.

Paint the Picture

I've learned lessons with examples of how to better use props to paint my picture for the audience that I will discuss later. Before you incorporate props, have you ever imagined your audience listening to your presentation with their eyes closed? Are you transporting them to another place and time? Are you providing relevant and descriptive details so they are able to visualize characters in your story?

Alternatively, are you providing too much detail? By this, I mean are you spending time on details that do not add value to your message or just aren't relevant? Will the audience care that the person you are describing wears red shoes? You need to ensure that the picture you're painting includes enough detail to set the tone, but doesn't waste precious time and energy on minor points that detract from the message you are trying to convey.

In addition, do the words and the delivery carry the emotions you want to evoke? My family and I like to watch the television show *American Idol* together. As singers compete, my wife comments that her judgment of a singer's performance varies depending on whether she is watching the television directly or is in a different room and only hearing the song. When she uses only her listening senses, she reacts differently because she can't see the wardrobe, the stage presence, and the lights on the singer. She often describes differences in passion and emotion coming from a singer based on the way the song is sung, emphasis on certain words, and passionate delivery she heard that I may not have noticed because I was caught up in the rest of the overall performance. The singer is painting a different picture for her due to the different perspective. The varying viewpoint painted a whole new picture for my wife.

I remember how my wife once described a singer who simply sang the words that were memorized, compared to the next singer who genuinely felt the words she was belting out. It was a potent lesson for me that I had to pay attention to various connection points I might have with my audience. I needed to paint a picture that would allow my audience to vividly see, even with their eyes closed. I had to provide the audience with the opportunity to take hold of the emotion I wanted them to feel. Even if the picture was slightly different from my own imagination, it should still create the emotion I wanted the audience to experience and thus make the message stick in their mind's eye.

26.

Formulate Clear Messages

It is imperative to state up front the message of intent of your speech to give the audience something to grasp. I once gave a speech with a surprise ending: the apparent "speaker" was actually my dog—the entire speech was from the perspective of my dog reading a letter to us, his owners. I chose not to let the audience in on the surprise as I meandered through the story. I forced the revelation onto the audience as my last action in the hopes of a climatic conclusion. It did not illicit the reaction I had intended. Using this speech in a Toastmasters club contest with only two other competitors, I finished in third place. The feedback I received was that although audiences like surprises, twists, and turns with storylines (these keep listeners interested and engaged), audiences rarely like having the walk-away message and theme sprung upon them with no warning.

Audiences enjoy surprises within a story, but they still want to understand how these surprises relate to the overall message. I found that waiting until the end, unfortunately, made my audience think too hard trying to guess the next twist or understand what I was trying to convey. Springing your message on a group at the end of your speech typically won't work; it becomes too heavy for the audience to absorb in one sitting. An audience wants the key points of a message supported with stories that become memorable days, weeks, and even months after the presentation.

My original dog story was nice, but rambled before it got to the eventual message I wanted the audience to absorb: to support adopting rescue animals. The message was also supposed to be simple. Unfortunately, it got lost in my attempt to surprise. The actual surprise was on me, because I lost my audience and never got them back. However, I was lucky enough to move on to the next competition because of scheduling conflicts for the other speakers, and I quickly revamped the introduction and body of the speech. I stopped worrying about surprising the audience and made the message obvious. This time, the audience was able to clearly see the intended message from the outset.

Once the audience had a chance to grasp the message, they could then enjoy the story and anecdotes more. The reinforced message left them with two actions to consider: either adopting a rescue animal or finding ways to support the Humane Society. The speech became one of my stronger competitive speeches, and I reached the Toastmasters District 45 Finals. I learned two lessons: First, clear messages and actions are a must for effective speeches. Audiences want to clearly understand the message as soon as possible and know what action is being asked of them. Second, the changes needed to make this happen are not as hard as you think. Go back to some of your past work, and see if a little re-working can change the whole presentation. The facelift I gave my original speech was simply a matter of reorganizing the structure with a clear message rather than rewriting the entire presentation.

27.

Reiterate and Reinforce Your Messages

My speech about the dog stuck with more people after the message was reinforced repeatedly. Audiences often need cadence and repeated information for a message to sink in. Whether a speaker uses pithy acronyms to make a message memorable, alliteration (e.g., "*r*aced home, *r*ipped open the bag, and *r*ealized..."), or requests soliciting responses, such as, "Repeat after me...," he or she needs to carry the intended message throughout the presentation. Retention of the information goes up considerably when the points are reiterated and reinforced. The stories used to support the message obviously can—and should—be different, but the message should continue to be crystal clear. The stories should take the audience on a clear, carefully linked path that leads them to the end. The message should be addressed in the opening, the body (several times), and the conclusion, to ensure that it carries the appropriate weight. As the back of your shampoo bottle says, "Rinse and repeat."

28.

Choose Your Words Carefully

Choose the words you want to use carefully. Maximize your impact by using words that put your thoughts in the best order, and select language that strengthens the sentence flow. You can ensure a clean transition between thoughts with the right vocabulary—words that the audience can relate to and absorb. The word choice, as you work on the speech order and the transitions, is critical in order to increase your effectiveness.

An often-made mistake, however, is looking to use big, intellectual words. The audience doesn't want to have their thoughts wander as they try to figure out word definitions. Select words that are easily understood and that convey the intended meaning. There are so many synonyms to choose from; just make sure they reflect the right definition for the point you want to make. Test the words out loud, check their flow, and then research the effectiveness of these word choices with smaller audiences, to see the reaction they get.

The words you choose for your speech should constantly evolve as the speech matures based on audience reactions, or in some cases, no reaction. Even when you are happy with a speech, it should be continually fine-tuned. Your words can have a lasting impact on your audience. They should be powerful enough to catch the audience's attention, but simple enough to be understood. If you think about news broadcasts, the anchors are using terminology for the masses. Unless you are presenting on a very specific or technical topic, make sure your word choices are used for impact, not just to sound smart. You will find that audiences often relate better to simple word choices.

28.

Have Clear Intentions

Before you sit down to write the greatest speech ever, go back to the basics. You can start with the seed. That seed may be a topic idea. Go back to your notebook and folder full of ideas (details will be discussed in an upcoming chapter). Now that you have something to work with, you are about to get to the part that may make or break the momentum of the entire speech. The next step should be deciding what you intend to do with that germinating idea. What is the objective of your speech? Do you want people to laugh, think, or cry? Do you want to persuade, motivate, inform, entertain, or inspire? You need to know the intended take-away for your audience *before* you begin the rest of the writing process. Once you've established how you would like the audience to react, you can then begin to outline the vision further.

If you just write your speech straight through without keeping your true intentions in mind, you will create more work for yourself as you refine it. You need to know how to transition effectively from a serious part of your speech to a more humorous one, for example. Having intentions in mind may also impact your word choice. If you just take your idea and run with it, you are not truly letting it germinate. Instead, try putting your idea in the middle of a piece of paper and brainstorming (by yourself and possibly with others), writing down everything that you think of about the idea. Your thoughts should come fast and furious, without being censored or developed; the extra effort of piecing them together comes later. This brainstorming may lead to the true path you want to take.

The most effective part of the exercise comes when you give yourself a time limit, such as fifteen minutes, to throw ideas together. Time pressure should keep the ideas flowing, without being over-engineered. The important part is that you are progressing down a path toward your message and theme intentions.

30.

Use Presentation Slides Effectively

I have been in one-hour presentations that have over one hundred slides. Now, wouldn't that get your attention with the question, "How does the presenter plan to get through all of this?" I've had many other questions that begin to float through my head as someone who will have to sit through this. The most common format for slide presentations is Microsoft PowerPoint. PowerPoint can be a strength or a hindrance, depending on the user. To most effectively use the tool, you must first understand that it is only a speaker's instrument and not the actual presentation. It will just sit there until it is brought to life by the presenter.

When planning how to integrate slides into your speech or presentation, you should start with the technical question of how they are going to be moved forward. Will you be the one controlling the movement, or will someone else be doing that? When possible, *you* should control the slides, to maintain the rhythm and timing you want. Each time you turn to someone else and say, "Next slide, please," it is one more potential distraction. Another major mistake made by the presenter is speaking with his or her head toward the slides. When you face the material you are talking about, you are turning yourself away from the audience; even if you have amplification, your back is typically toward the group. You are there to speak to the audience, not the slides. I know this sounds obvious and a little snippy, but it happens far too often, and you need to realize that you should continue to look forward when using slides.

In addition, if the font is large enough to read, give your audience some credit that they can see what is on the screen and you don't need to read the slide line for line. Give the audience the appropriate context and points of emphasis, and remember that nothing tears you apart from your audience more quickly than condescendingly reading verbatim.

Many PowerPoint presenters attempt to get overly elaborate with the slide content and visuals. I, like many audience members, am a simple person who wants to see a simple message. If your message gets lost in the fancy pictures, arrows and symbols, you have disengaged yourself from both your intended message and the audience.

Finally, the best plans do go awry, so have a back-up plan. Can you do your presentation without slides, or are you too dependent? If the answer is that the slides are the focal point of the entire presentation, re-tool your presentation so the slides are supportive only. Be prepared in case the slides don't work. You might even surprise yourself at how much more engaged your audience will be and how much more effective your message is delivered without them.

31.

End Strong

As an audience member, have you ever started to gather your things together and gotten ready to stand up following a presentation that didn't really end? You may have been given cues, such as "In conclusion…," "Finally," and "As I wrap this up," but the presentation keeps going. The audience must not be left guessing when your presentation is to be wrapped up. The presenter should ensure that there is a nice, tidy bow wrapped up on the conclusion. In the business world, I see this happen at the end of presentations, and even conference calls, where the host is not sure how to end, so we get minutes of filler and babbling while the listeners begin preparation for their next call or activity. I suggest being simple and confident. For a call, you may say, "Thank you for your contributions on the call, and have a great day." For a presentation, you may say, "The final point is to…," and end with, "Thank you for being a great audience." Everyone will know it is over.

The key to success is your ability as a speaker to exude confidence that everything is wrapped up. Your conclusion should be a summation of what you told them, with emphasis on the critical points you want the group to walk away with. Never assume the audience caught everything. A strong recap reinforces the messages and ends the presentation on a potentially motivating, inspiring, or action-specific note. Find an effective way to *end it*. Don't recap your recap and keep talking. After the summation, come in strongly and clearly and wrap it up.

32.

Reinforce Three Times, Three Times, Three Times

Whether it was from reading about public speaking, public-speaking training, or through points emphasized by professional speakers everywhere, the often cited "Rule of Three" in speaking is a tool that can be used often and effectively. This rule is important to the rhythm of the message, the sentence structure, and the cadence. The natural flow of using three examples to emphasize your points, such as "He was thirsty, hungry, and tired," allows you to begin to paint the picture clearly and concisely. Not every sentence in your speech or presentation needs three examples, but periodically embedding threes into the message gives it a splash of continuity.

Additionally, the power of three comes into play when making supported points throughout the body of the speech. The audience can't remember all of the critical details. Even in short speeches, if they are given a plethora of messages to remember, the human mind can only retain so much information. A useful speech technique is to frame a strong opening followed by three points you want to make, each supported with a story or example, followed by a solid summary. The use of three examples is a tested tool that consistently takes hold with all audiences.

33.

Recycle Your Own Work

T he fourth Toastmasters speech I ever wrote for Toastmasters had a pithy little title: "Chinese Takeout." I wrote it as part of my journey through the required projects designed to methodically improve communication skills. While I was giving the speech, there were a couple of chuckles, and one member suggested that I should enter it into the annual Humorous Speech Contest. I delivered it exactly as I had written it for the club contest. I successfully progressed in the competition through the next couple of levels. I was lucky to progress to these levels, because the top *two* competitors moved on, and I was consistently finishing second. I was new to the process and just happy to keep succeeding. I remember saying to myself that I could never beat the winning speech. What I really meant was that I was too close to the event and too inexperienced to understand the fluidity of the process.

Two years later, I remembered the speech and thought I would take another look. I reread it and again found myself chuckling at a couple of parts. I did have mixed emotions, though. I was simultaneously upset and excited. I was upset because I saw far too many places in the original speech that needed to be revamped and improved, and I was excited because I realized that it was an early speech, from a time when I was less experienced. Even though there was so much to change, the baseline story was solid.

If you've ever had writer's block, go back to something you've already done and you'll find that you can, and should, freshen up your own work. There is no need to invent something brand new every time you set out to speak.

34.

Use What Works — and Reuse to Meet Your Needs

Reuse what has already worked for you. In the last section we mentioned a recycled speech; however, here I am broadening the scope to include experiences, stories, jokes, and anecdotes that have gotten some type of rise or reaction from people. Whether they were co-workers, family, or friends, if you touched one person with a comment or story, there is a good likelihood that you can touch many others. Try it out, and see if it works. Too many presenters try to invent something brand new for their audiences and come up against across writer's block.

We can reuse only so much of our lives. Since the best connection to an audience is sharing something personal, go back and revisit the folder and file in which you keep your stash of treasures. The key is to use a story in a way that will connect with the audience and still serve your purpose to entertain, inspire, or motivate. You can use the same story to be funny or to be serious, depending on the environment, the audience, and the message you want to send. I have a speech about my shy oldest daughter who stepped out on stage at a school concert to sing solo. There are so many places I use the story. I have used a funny line about how I needed to talk to her about the little white lies she was told us prior to the event to keep the surprise, I have noted how much courage she had that I had never seen before, and I have used it for motivational purposes as an example of stepping out of one's comfort zone. I can keep going, but my point is that there are many messages to the same story. If it works, find a use for it.

35.

Set Your Stage Story

I watched Joey Grondin at the 2009 Fall Division B Toastmasters conference present on "Developing Your Signature." I will never forget some of his key points because he set me up, as an audience member, to remember his stories through his "stage location." He talked about how all of a speaker's movements should be intentional, stopping at specific places on the stage so people would relate those places to different parts of the story, thus helping them remember the message.

Sometimes, a speaker paces back and forth, which simply makes the audience's eyes follow the speaker back and forth. The constant movement may be distracting enough to be remembered more than the key points. Joey emphasized the need to set the story up. You may be walking and talking, and then at a point of emphasis in the story, you can "anchor" yourself at a section of the stage. Each part of the stage—including the whole depth, not just the front—can be used to share new stories and messages. The audience will remember the story relative to where the speaker was on stage when he or she made the poignant point.

36.

Know That Less is More

I have always considered myself detail-oriented and liked to share these details regardless of the audience. I consistently have to remind myself to "know the audience" in order to determine how much detail to include in a presentation, especially in business. Is it an executive summary or an in-depth analysis? The amount of detail will vary based on the audience needs. However, Ed Tate, the 2000 Toastmaster World Champion, seemed to speak directly to me at the 2010 District 45 Fall Conference when he said, "Less is more."

I felt as though I had been making strides in my business presentations by sticking to the key points; however, this was harder for me to grasp in my non-business-related speeches. I found myself giving intimate details about a person, possibly even including what he or she was wearing. Although "painting the picture" is critical, it must be carefully crafted so that the audience can formulate their own thoughts and descriptions. Ed's point was to give the audience enough to begin to use their own imagination to paint a picture without detracting from the story and message. If you are discussing an event, details like the trip to get there may be irrelevant if they don't connect to the main point. Eliminating immaterial background information will enhance the critical parts of the story. Less detail will create more of an impact if done correctly.

37.

Make Writing a Habit

Increase the power of your words by strengthening your writing skills. This comes with writing every day. I know this for a fact. I presented my first book, *The Transformation of a Doubting Thomas: Growing from a Cynic to a Professional in the Corporate Environment*, to my literary agent and was so proud of my work. However, I found I was more proud of saying I was done. Then, I put together the proposal and received some rejections from publishers. When we decided to resubmit the work to other publishers, I wanted to re-read my work. I was still proud, but realized how much stronger the writing was in the latter part of the book. My writing became obviously stronger as the book progressed. I went back and strengthened the weaker sections. I found I became a much better writer simply by writing each day. The same is true for your speeches and presentations: The more you write and test your material, the more in tune you will be with your strengths and the audience's wants and needs.

38.

Give Numbers Context

I often hear statistics tossed out in speeches as a way to grab the audience's attention. However, numbers can be risky if they are left alone. Let me share an example. In a speech about animal euthanasia, I stated, "Each year, six to eight million animals are euthanized in shelters across America." The number "six to eight million" can be either large or small, depending on the context. It sounds like a lot, but there is very little for the audience to grab hold of beyond the number itself, which can easily be forgotten and its impact potentially lost. I did some additional research and was able to find out that this number was similar in size to some other large numbers that I could compare it to. I was able to hook the audience into remembering the estimates by simply adding the following line: "Did you realize the high end of that estimate is the same as the population of New York City?" Give a number some contextual teeth to make it memorable.

39.

Let the Speech Breathe

I learned a valuable lesson by hiding a speech from my wife. It was not the lesson you might be thinking of if you thought that withholding it was what got me in trouble with her. I had a five-hour drive coming home from a Toastmasters convention. I was inspired and had ideas racing though my head. I actually sent myself voicemails to ensure the ideas were not forgotten. I came up with a humorous speech called, "The Wife Coach."

I told my wife about the events leading up to the concept but held off on sharing the full speech because I wasn't sure if it was ready yet. I obviously wanted to get some laughs, but not at her expense, so I had to be delicate in my writing. I actually put it away for about six months. I brought it on vacation in the summer to begin work on it again, and shared it with close friends. They saw the humor but made some suggestions. What was interesting is that what I thought was hilarious when first written, didn't quite hit as hard after I gave it time to settle. I made new revisions with my close friends, and finally my wife, and again received critical feedback. The valuable lesson of letting the speech breathe allowed me to bring a much stronger version to the Division B Toastmasters finals (for the state of Maine and parts of New Hampshire). I had roaring laughter at some parts, enough to lead to my first paid speaking engagement.

40.

Tell the Audience
What You Just Told Them

The old adage of telling them what you are going to tell them, telling them, and then telling them what you just told them stands the test of time and is critical in delivering a memorable speech. Telling the audience something that goes over their head or won't be remembered can be a waste of time and energy for everyone involved. Make sure that the intended key points stick with the audience so that they spring into action or retain your message far after the presentation. When structuring the speech, repeat the message throughout the work, including in the introduction, body, and conclusion.

However, repeating messages is not the only tool. You can use creative means, such as props, to keep the audience's attention; ask open-ended questions of the audience to repeat back key messages; or have the group write it down. However, in all of these examples we are assuming that the message stuck. Another adage *never assume* also stands strong. Reiterate points you want them to walk away with in a clearly laid-out manner to ensure that the audience gets *exactly* what you want them to get. Audiences interpret what was told to them in many ways. When you restate the key points in an organized and summarized manner, you have a better chance that they will sink in at a deeper level.

The Audience

41.

Look Each Audience Member in the Eye

We often look *over* the audience and *through* the audience. I have been known to dart my eyes quickly between audience members or even look down at the floor. Audiences want a connection with the speaker. In addition to a message they can relate to, they want to feel as though you are talking directly to them. Take the time to make recognizable eye contact with each person in the audience. This includes people in the front and all the way in the back. Even if you, the speaker, are in a spotlight on stage, make the effort to reach out with your eyes to the last person in the last row. Even if you don't actually connect visually with the person in the last row, the feeling of intimate connection will be there.

42.

Project Your Voice

You have worked too hard writing, rehearsing, and preparing to let any words be wasted. Your voice is an obvious tool in any public-speaking event. As important as it is to use voice fluctuation to improve audience engagement, it is just as important to enunciate words and project your voice for the world to hear. I am not talking about yelling or always maintaining high volume, but the vocals should come from deep in the gut so your audience can hear everything you have to say. When practicing, have people sit in different parts of the room to ensure that your voice is projected appropriately. Try turning your head in different directions and testing your projection to ensure you are still heard everywhere in the room. As a reminder, voice projection comes in addition to the varying volumes you want to use during your presentation in order to keep the audience's attention. The key point is that the voice should not be sustained at a soft tone or whisper throughout the presentation. Don't make your audience strain to hear you.

43.

Appeal to Audience Interests

Audiences are, and should be, selfish. We often hear the phrase, "What's in it for me?" Forcing what you believe on an audience does not help you relate to their wants and needs. Even if you are attempting to persuade them to take your point of view, you still need points and counterpoints that will appeal to them. Depending on the setting, if provided the opportunity, ask the meeting organizer or potential attendees about their interests prior to the event. If you can share an anecdote or story about someone in the audience who is well known to other audience members, or cover a topic that many of the audience members have experienced, you will broaden your appeal. In the business of public speaking, many speakers employ a pre-meeting questionnaire to be filled out on audience demographics, likes, dislikes, and taboo topics. Any information you can gather ahead of time will add value to the intent of the presentation because the audience will see what's in it for them.

44.

Make the Speech about Them, Not You

When we start as inexperienced speakers, our first thoughts naturally turn inward toward ourselves. We worry if we will look good, if we will say the right things, and if we will meet our own goals. The self-centered view is a perfectly normal first step in the public-speaking continuum. We want to look good and not embarrass ourselves. First thoughts are always self-centered.

It is acceptable to start this way as you work on your comfort zone; however, your biggest breakthrough will be the moment you start speaking for the people in front of you. Your every move and every thought should be geared toward earning respect and trust, and establishing a relationship with the people in the seats. When your preparation and actions start revolving around those listening to you, you find a greater connection. You, personally, will see a difference in how you present yourself with respect to your passion and energy. You should ask, rhetorically, "What can I do for you?" The different answers from an audience-centered view may surprise you.

45.

Appreciate the Audience's
Diversity and Differences

As previously stated, your whole presentation should be geared toward an audience's interests and needs. Have you asked yourself and the organizer the right questions to ensure that you respect and value the full makeup of the audience? Diversity can relate to some of the more common topics such as race, gender, ethnicity, and age, as well as socio-economic status, educational levels, differing opinions, and different levels of knowledge on certain subjects. All of these differences have to be accounted for within a presentation. Speakers are often told to stay away from controversial and contentious topics (unless it is a targeted audience and topic), including religion and politics. For the most part, this is sound advice. However, in addition to political and religious views, you need to clearly recognize the differences among your audience members. By doing this, you will instantly add credibility and value to what you are trying to accomplish. For example, simply *asking* an audience to speed you up if they are familiar with a subject or to slow you down if they need more time to absorb shows your flexibility and inclusivity. When you create an environment where everyone feels welcome, you increase your ability to relate, thus increasing the chances that the audience will appreciate the intended message. As a spectator, even if I don't agree with the message, I will at least respect it and understand that it is the opinion of the speaker.

46.

Know What They Want

"They" in this case is the organizer and the people who will be attending the function. Do you know if what you plan to say matches the theme of the overall program, convention, or event, or have you made assumptions? You should ask these questions ahead of time, to prepare yourself for the event: How long do I have? What time do I go on? Who is introducing me? Is the audience expecting humor? Is it a keynote address, or is it supposed to be educational? Is it a lecture, and how interactive is the audience expecting it to be?

When speaking with the meeting organizer, you need to get a preview of what to expect. If the answer from the organizer is, "I don't know," then some homework has to be done by one or both of you. Do you know what the expected attendance is? Have you asked if other speakers will be there, since this could influence order and flow? As the speaker, have you done your own research on the organization? Is it possible to integrate some key pieces of information, like the organization's history, into your presentation in order to establish an instant connection? Once you figure out what "they" want, then adjust your presentation accordingly.

47.

Be an Attentive Audience Yourself

When you are an audience member, be a critical observer of the speaker. Watch the speaker's body movement, gestures, and stage presence, and listen for voice inflections (changes in pitch and tone). What is the speaker doing right that is keeping your attention and engaging you? Even harder, what can be improved if he or she is losing your attention? Is there something distracting about the mannerisms, use of language, or lack of passion? Are you beginning to count the number of distracting filler words, such as "um," "ah," "you know," and "like," and is the speaker ending every sentence with "really?" and "right?!" Is the message obvious and carried through the presentation? Are there supporting stories? Is it believable? Has the speaker gained your trust and respect, and come across as genuine? You can focus on your own opportunities and target your observations of the speaker. For example, if you have trouble being concise put your critical-listening skills into play and see if the speaker is using an economy of words. You should also take notes for reference later. As a consummate observer, you will always be in learning mode, therefore in a constant state of improvement.

48.

Work on Your
"Um, Ya Know" Filler Words

As much as I might want to say I have never said "um," "ah," "ya know," and "to be honest with you," I would be lying. Yes, "to be honest with you" is another potentially distracting filler phrase that I have used. We all unnecessarily fill silence and voids with non-descript words that have little to no meaning. Even the word "awesome" has lost its true meaning with its overuse. My recent favorite is with the habit of many people ending their sentences with, "Right?" The painful, but effective, solution to filler words is to become conscious of your saying them. Whether you have some trusted listeners around you who will count them or throw a hand up when you say them, or you become conscious of your own usage, you will find that simply paying attention to them and making a concerted effort to improve is all you need to break the habit. We have a comfort level with the use of some of these so-called words and phrases and have built a habit that has to be broken. Just as you would do kicking any bad habit, exercise a strong will, find a solid support system, and you will improve.

49.

Engage Your Audience

Engaging and connecting with your audience can be as easy as asking questions. Rhetorical, closed-ended questions, such as "Have you ever found yourself in a similar situation...?" will get the audience thinking and heads potentially nodding. You can up the ante with more thought-provoking questions, such as, "What if you found yourself with one day left to live?" The audience instantly will start to relate by figuring out what's in it for them. It is imperative to find creative ways to make the audience a part of the speech somehow by understanding how your words relate to them. Asking thought-provoking open or closed-ended questions allows the door to open to appeal to the audience wants and needs, even when a direct audience response isn't needed.

Conversely, you can interact with the audience by asking them questions that need may require a reply. There is the obvious and often overused question: "How's everyone doing today?" Or you can ask everyone to stand up and get involved somehow. All of these examples avoid letting your audience be passive, and begins to make them a part of the event. Be creative to engage your audience.

50.

Have an Individual Conversation with the Whole Audience

When you're giving a presentation, it should come across as naturally as a dinner conversation with a loved one. The topics may be slightly different, but the tone should not be. The audience should feel as though they are in your living room with you having a nice chat, so that you come across as genuine, thus providing sincerity and credibility. If the audience feels as though you are acting, or you are speaking *through* them (instead of *with* them), you will lose them. Your true personality will begin to shine only when you adopt a conversational approach. This doesn't mean you can't use tools like voice inflection and stage presence, but having the audience perceive your presentation as a personal conversation will strengthen their bond with you.

51.

Reduce Personal Distractions

Change jingling in the pocket or even a cell phone strapped to your side can take the focus off you and distract the audience just enough to miss your message. Work badges hanging from your side swaying back and forth can have the same effect. Prior to speaking, remove lapel pins and any badges ("Hello my name is…"), pagers and cell phones, and any potentially swinging jewelry. The goal is to minimize the possibility of distractions before it is too late. It seems so small, but any distraction taking away from your message is important to address, especially when the solutions are so simple.

52.

Make the Message Stick

Audiences learn and retain information differently. My youngest daughter can sit back and absorb a presentation without taking a note and repeat back everything—and I mean *everything*—she heard. Others, like me, are consummate note-takers. Still others may need some type of visual or auditory stimulation to retain information. It is important to understand this learning diversity when preparing your presentation. Depending on the type of presentation, if possible provide multiple options that work best for information retention by various learning types.

As a speaker, you must have an engaged audience. You can capture their attention by getting them involved, possibly by having them out of their seats to complete an action, or asking open-ended questions that need responses. Additionally, you can have the audience repeat key points you want emphasized or remembered. For some learners, you should provide handouts; many of these learners want something to hold and read from or want to fill in the blanks. Providing paper and a place to take notes makes a big difference to someone like me. Finally, you have people who sit on their hands until they see a visual on the screen or hear music in the background. It's important to account for these visual and auditory learners. More importantly, it's essential to show flexibility for different learners in your audience. The message sticks more when you are conscientious about your audience's needs and learning types.

53.

Don't Talk about Your Bad Day

We have all had bad days, whether we are not feeling so hot, didn't sleep well, or forgot to pick up the bread our significant other asked for (sorry, honey). These days happen. However, in the public-speaking forum, your audience most likely doesn't care. In fact, you are giving your credibility a backseat to the messages you want to send if you start your presentation with, "Please give me sympathy, or at least understand that I'm not giving you my 'A' game." You shouldn't announce it or even show it in your non-verbal cues. You can't afford to lose your audience. Never start a speech with an apology. Make the effort to muscle through whatever it is and set a better tone right from the beginning. You may be surprised to find that the audience's energy, which you are helping to create, may just solve whatever problem you were having anyway.

54.

Avoid Side Comments

Avoid side comments that may detract from your presentation. Any comment not specific to your message takes attention away from what you are trying to accomplish as a speaker. To an audience member, side comments may be seen as a potential loss of focus, attention given to someone or something that doesn't need it, or a lack of confidence. Let me give some examples:

Loss of focus: Asking someone to get the lights or asking, "Is my microphone working?" can become your unintended introduction once everyone is settled.

Lack of preparation: Asking if everyone received the packet of information handed out may give an indication of a lack of preparation. Why weren't these packets handed out before the presentation? I have learned that people will most often ask for something if they did not get it.

Misdirected attention: When someone comes in late and you acknowledge that person it takes away from the guests who were there on time.

Lack of confidence or lost credibility: Avoid telling the world that you lack confidence and avoid giving any indication that can lose your audience's trust. You can instantly lose credibility by saying that you are nervous, that you are not ready, that this isn't your line of expertise, that you didn't have much time to prepare, that you are long-winded, that the audience may be bored with a section of the presentation, and many other comments. All of these are real examples that are heard often, especially with less-experienced speakers. If any of the previously mentioned excuses are accurate, rally through them and don't announce them. More importantly, do all of the practice and preparation possible to avoid the need to make side comments in the first place.

Ideas and Presentation

55.

Brainstorm:
The Friends-and-Family Effect

Who knows you better, outside of yourself, than your friends, family, and colleagues? When you are searching for topics or trying to fine-tune a passionate presentation, invest time with the people closest to you. Throw ideas against the wall and see if they stick. Use the close relationships to ensure that the messages you want to convey truly come across as intended. You should not fear feedback because of the comfort in realizing that if this group of people can't provide you with the gift of their honest opinions, then who can? It is impossible to do it alone.

I spent the first year and a half after joining Toastmasters practicing my speeches in the car and in front of mirrors. Although both are good tools, they can't compare to the eyes of your spouse or significant other staring back at you. I learned that if I could do it well in front of my wife, then a couple hundred people would be easy. I finally shared a competition speech with my wife right before I got in the car to drive to the competition. The speech typically took six and a half minutes to perform. For her, I did it in five minutes because of my anxiety, since I really wanted to impress her. Within the speech, I had the line, "Millions of dogs and cats"; instead, I said, "Millions of dogs and a cat." We laughed together after the speech. I knew she was a supporter of my public speaking, but didn't realize how much I could rely on her. After I became more comfortable with my dependence on her, I learned to have healthier dialogues regarding subjective feedback. In another speech, I had the line, "My first legal adult beverage…," and my wife said it was too obscure and lacked the punch I wanted. She suggested using, "My first beer…." I fought her on it until a friend suggested the exact same line. Somehow, I had known she was right, but I had refused to listen (I still have work to do in listening to my wife). I have now become an open book to friends and family, especially to my greatest supporter, my wife.

56.

Keep a Notebook Nearby

Ask me what I had for dinner last night and there is a really good chance I won't remember. Not many of us can easily come up with what we ate without really thinking about it. Now think of the greatest speech idea you ever had, but can't remember. How many times have you been driving down the road or woken up in the middle of the night thinking, "Wow, I need to remember that," or, "I should do a speech on that," or some other iteration, then kept on driving or fell back to sleep and never remembered what it was? The easiest way to solve that problem is with a notebook or folder nearby. I keep a notebook on my nightstand and a folder in my laptop bag, which is typically always near me. I simply jot the idea down and toss the paper back. It can be one word or a short sentence. Write down whatever is enough for you to remember. Notice I didn't say write out the entire speech. You can let the idea stew and grow in your mind while it's in the notebook or folder. The idea will continue to nurture and develop itself over time. Go back to it when it is time, and start outlining the message and content. You will be shocked how easily the speech flows because your mind has been running in the background with this topic, simply because you wrote it down.

57.

Research Your Material

I realize I am stating the obvious, but we are lucky to be surrounded with so many tools, like the Internet, to research our material, and it seems so natural to use these tools to strengthen our messages. The benefits of research range from keeping your material current, to ensuring that it is accurate and not trademarked by others. If you are a frequent speaker on the same topic, ask yourself when you last updated your material. Pay attention to your information, and keep it timely by scanning relevant websites, news media, and books. I used to tell a story about the word "chillax," a made-up combination of "chill out" and "relax." Over time, I found that the impact waned as the use of the word dwindled in popular culture. Besides keeping you and me up to date, researching even simple facts may yield further information for expanding your material or creating spinoffs to existing information. As obvious as it is, don't forget to use the tools that are at your disposal to research your material to strengthen your message.

58.

Be a Secret (or Not So Secret) Admirer

There are plenty of people we look up to. Whether it is a family member or a historical figure, we get strength from the success of others. The same should be said for people who speak well. If people you know—from work, from an organization, or simply from crossing paths—have a skill you want to work on, try to find an opportunity to connect with them formally or informally. If you can seek them out as a mentor or find ways to at least get some tips from them to improve yourself, it will make you stronger. You don't want to admire from afar when it comes to improving your public-speaking skills. I have found that successful people in the field tend to be open and supportive in sharing suggestions. You should take in everything that will continue your positive learning trajectory. Clearly, we should not go about it independently. We need support and help along the way for our continued growth.

I have connected with many great speakers who produce routine newsletters, and have found formal and informal mentors who have shared what they do well with me. These little things begin to add up to a much greater success when we start to implement their feedback. Even if you don't know someone personally, are there other ways to connect with him or her? Can you connect with the person through

LinkedIn or through other professional groups? Do you go online and read well-known speeches and analyze them or even attend a webinar? You can go to YouTube, Google, or other websites to find great speeches and great speakers who can meet your needs. Do you take a unique learning perspective to see the strengths of the speech structure and purpose? Can you easily understand the intended message? Finding individual speakers whom you can emulate and learn from should inspire you to reach further and perfect your craft. Finding the right connections and immersing yourself in their teaching can only make your own presentations stronger.

59.

Practice – This is Not an Option

If you are giving a prepared speech, then ensure that it *is* prepared. You can't check over notes right before you go on to present and consider that preparation. You should practice in front of family, friends, cats, and dogs. Find anyone and anything to be in front of to ensure that you have practiced more than just the words. You should practice pacing, voice inflections and places to pause, stage usage, and physical aspects of the speech. There is too much left to chance without preparation.

There is no such thing, in my opinion, as too much practice. There is some risk of too much of a staged presentation, so you should use caution to make sure your movements remain natural. However, practice is required to get better. When practicing for speeches, if I am listening to the radio in the car, I practice during commercials, or if I am transitioning between tasks at work, I may find a few minutes to run through a speech or presentation. The amount of positive feedback I continue to receive about my obvious improvement in confidence and skills is validation enough to keep practicing.

60.

Be a Student of Yourself

Only you control the final touches you will make to the presentation. After receiving feedback from anyone and everyone, don't forget the most important person to get feedback from: yourself. Be a student of yourself. Use the simple tools of a mirror or a video camera to improve in all aspects of speaking, whether it is speech content, delivery, stage usage, non-verbal gestures, voice inflection, or the many other facets. Video is often difficult for people to accept as a valuable tool, probably because it says so much. To see, hear, and analyze ourselves is tough because most people are harder on themselves than on anyone else, due to the pursuit of perfection.

Once you get past the uneasiness of watching yourself, you will immediately see the benefits of video because you can rewind and watch it multiple times for further reinforcement. More importantly, you can target the feedback for yourself. When you review the video, break it down by isolating certain aspects. For example, turn off the sound. Because you no longer need your hearing senses for this part of the exercise, you will make crucial observations about the non-verbal and physical aspects of the speech that you might well have missed otherwise. Invest time to be critical of yourself and you will be amazed at how much you transform. The ability to study yourself drives home the best in you because who knows you more than you?

61.

Practice Through to the End

When I first started learning the piano, at the late age of thirty-eight, my passionate piano teacher drove into my head that when I hit the wrong note, I should keep playing through to the end. She emphasized that if I stopped every time I made a mistake, I would never make it to the last note. I would suggest the same with a speech, once it is ready to practice in its entirety. You need to get it ingrained in your head that you will not be perfect. You will make mistakes, and that is a fact. When you stop at the point of the mistake, you will hurt the flow and also probably influence how you react in the middle of a real presentation if you make a mistake; you may be creating a habit of stopping where you are and starting over, which will not be good for you or the audience.

As you go back to certain sections and repeat them over and over, you are fine-tuning portions of the presentation but limiting your ability to look at the speech holistically. There is more to a speech than just content. Flow and rhythm are built throughout, and stopping each time you make a mistake makes them harder to recognize. In some of my earlier speech practice habits, I started over again whenever I made a mistake. This made the beginning of the speech flawless because I had said it so many times. There have been times, because of the added pressure of the actual performance, where I lost my place in the body of the speech that had been practiced less. I surprised myself with mistakes I had never made before in practice. I am convinced it was because I did not take my piano teacher's advice. I have made considerably fewer mistakes since I have learned to practice all the way through.

62.

Practice with Distractions

I once was in a Toastmasters divisional-level speech contest (for the state of Maine and parts of New Hampshire), when out of the blue came the boisterous noise of a jackhammer. The floor was thumping and rattling, and my concentration was shot. I became flustered and made several mistakes. After the contest, I analyzed my practice routine leading up to the event: I would clear the room of any distractions, put the dog outside, and close the doors for complete silence. In a perfect world, this made sense. How do you prepare for an unexpected baby crying (I've had this happen, too), papers rustling, or silverware and glasses clanking? As a speaker, you can only control so much.

I began practicing with distractions everywhere. I have practiced with the television and radio on. I have invited the dog in and stepped over him on more than one occasion. I have forged ahead in my speech when the phone rang. My favorite was practicing while my ten-year-old daughter began her brand-new trombone lessons. Yes, it does sound like a bunch of elephants, but the distraction challenge is beautiful. You will become more nimble in your surroundings if you prepare for anything. Your concentration level, having been put to the test, will make you ready for the distractions you can't predict.

63.

Write Out Key Points

Y ou will want to emphasize key points with the audience, but in the excitement of the presentation, the risk of leaving out one or more of these key points is real. Have the messages you want the audience to remember in an easily accessible spot to review before the presentation, during the presentation, and at the conclusion, to ensure that all pertinent points are covered. It is easy to get caught up in a discussion or even go down a different path based on the interaction with the audience, so it is important that the points you want taken away are there to reference, to ensure that they are not forgotten.

These points should be written out, bolded, underlined, and reiterated throughout your outline and eventual speech. They are the focal points of the presentation, so you should also have indicators written out for *how* you want the points to be made. Delivery of these points can be critical in how your message is received and retained. Your cue may be adding it to the story you want the point to support, repeating the line, increasing your volume, or slowing down intentionally. You don't necessarily need to script out every move you make, although this might be a good habit early in your speaking evolution. The key is to ensure that your points resonate with the audience. The goal is to build muscle memory through practice so that the key points become so natural that the audience will be scrambling for their notebooks, saying, "Why didn't I think of that?" Good muscle memory starts with a good plan.

64.

Add Value with Your Visual Aids

I have consistently been coached to find my unique and differentiating factors and to emphasize them during presentations. For example, I have the luxury of having low-cost, professional posters available. I was convinced that these posters would become my way to be remembered. As a frequent presenter with these posters, I was receiving positive feedback. I found my use of them got to a point of dependency. I wouldn't necessarily call it lazy with my writing, but my incorporation of the props became a focal point, thus a distraction from the main messages. I learned as a speech contestant that I would receive rave reviews in the early stages because judges often thought the posters were a nice touch and separated me from other competitors. As I progressed further in the competitions, so did the judges. Their experience level typically increased and they wanted a picture to be painted vividly with words, not an *actual* picture. In a key competition, I excitedly turned a poster around from its blank-white back to the high-school yearbook picture of a friend of mine who had passed away. I lost the competition.

After losing, I received some feedback that although the poster was nice, many people thought it took away from my message. Obviously, I had leaned on my prop as a principle focus instead of just as a supporting tool. Some feedback also indicated that right from the start the audience was guessing what was on the front of the poster, so I was losing their attention before I had even started. At the point when I turned the poster around, it hit the stand slightly. Although subtle to me, apparently the distraction was bigger in the eyes of the judges because they saw the risk ahead of time, and I fulfilled their prophecy. The most important feedback given to me on that day was that the line I delivered in the speech before I turned the picture around— "He was four-foot-eleven with a five-foot smile"— had described in words everything people needed to envision this person properly on their own. Unfortunately, I showed them the movie immediately after they had just read the book. Whatever picture they had in their own mind was instantly ruined. It was as if I had just stolen the audience's imagination. Finally, I was told that the audience at times felt my stage presence was hindered or even predictable because the props dictated where I was going on stage. Thus, the supporting props had become a distraction.

I may have lost the competition, but I guess I really won going forward if such caring people were willing to provide me substantial, easy-to-act-on feedback. I learned a lot that day about ensuring that visual aids and props *support* the message, but don't take away from it.

65.

Grab Attention with Your Opening

"Hello. My name is Tom Dowd. How are you doing today? Today we are going to talk about (insert boring topic introduction here)...." How many presentations have you heard with this type of canned opening? It is a mainstay in business presentations. Don't lose your audience before you truly get started. Avoid telling them what you plan to do until you have already grabbed their attention. We have most likely been taught to tell audiences what we want to tell them, tell them and then rehash what we have just told them. Sometimes, we are so literal that the introduction becomes, "I am going to tell you about blah blah blah...," which I have heard too often delivered monotone, with no voice inflection.

Just dive in with your attention-grabbing introduction. You can tell them what you are about to tell them, but get their attention first. I have shocked more than one concerned audience when I've broken into a coughing fit as an introduction to an inspirational speech about a childhood friend with cystic fibrosis. Start a speech with a song, a bang, a powerful quote, or a question that demands an immediate response. There are so many more creative openings than "Hello, my name is...." Your audience should be in for a surprise. You can give them one from the start. It will set the tone for the rest of the presentation.

66.

Remember Audio-Visual Equipment Needs

Preparation is critical to avoid any mishaps with AV equipment. Do you have an extra light bulb for your projector? Let's even take a step back and ask if you have your own projector. Will you need to bring one? What about extension cords and screens? You can't leave anything to chance, you can't *assume* when it comes to delivering the best presentation. Have you physically been to the room where you are going to present ahead of time? The preparation is not just walking in a few minutes before the event. It is crucial that you talk with the meeting organizer ahead of time and walk the stage well in advance. I recommend when practicing on the actual stage that you give a large portion of the speech, if not all, ahead of time using the live AV equipment. Saying, "Test 1, 2, 3" into a microphone does not count as preparation.

Have you walked around the entire stage to ensure there are no extra-sensitive feedback spots for the microphones? Your audience will appreciate not hearing any high-pitched squeaks. I have a loud voice naturally, so I also invest a lot of time testing the volume of the microphones. You should also work with the organizers ahead of time on microphone options. I personally prefer lapel or the ones connected to the ear with the speaker near the mouth because I like to use my hands, and for me it is worth asking ahead of time for one of these.

Have you emailed your material to the organizer? Are paper copies ready and waiting in case of an AV failure, or can the material be projected in another way? Do you have a thumb drive, just in case something goes wrong with the organizer's version? I know I am at my best when I have tested and prepared for everything I can control; therefore, my audience's ability to receive my message should go up. Finally, expect the unexpected. It is not a matter of "if" something will go wrong, it is "when" it will go wrong. Part of your preparation should revolve around how flexible your presentation is *without* the audio-visual equipment in case it doesn't work.

67.

Manage Phone Presentations Well

As part of a very large company, I have been asked to present many times over the phone. These conversations have advantages and disadvantages. Let's start with some of the advantages. You can surround yourself with notes and not worry about being as discreet as you would have to when in front of large audiences. You can also typically have more control over the flow of the conversation.

However, one pitfall is not being able to physically observe audience reactions, which makes it more difficult to adjust the presentation mid-stream. You may be able to hear some laughter, sighs, or groans, but what happens when the phones are on mute and all you hear is silence? You may need to adapt your style, asking for more engagement—to make sure you have kept the audience's attention—through verbal responses or, on webcasts and meetings with the appropriate platform, through voting-type buttons for opinions or answers. You also may have the inverse, when a phone is not on mute but the listeners have chosen to multi-task and you hear keyboards clicking, phone conversations, dogs barking or, worse, personal information you wish you hadn't heard. As a speaker, you should set expectations ahead of time, such as whether you would like the presentation to be interactive or have the audience hold questions and answers until the end. You can ask that everyone put their phones on mute, if needed. You should also know whom to contact to disconnect a distracting line, if possible.

Finally, you need to ensure that the presentation itself is adaptable to the phone. The first professional development conversation I did for a large group of people over the phone was a flop. I did not change it from my dynamic face-to-face presentation, so my use of the stage became irrelevant, and my gestures were useless. I had to depend more on open and inviting questions for the audience and more on voice inflection to share my passion. The phone can reach a wider audience and be just as impactful, as long as you know that some revisions and varying preparation are required for the best outcome.

68.

Test Your Speeches

As previously mentioned, friends and family are always great sources of feedback for your speeches. However, nothing beats the local flavor of a group of people who may not be as close to the subject as your friends and family. I can't thank enough the local support I have received from Rotary Clubs, Kiwanis Clubs, Lions Clubs, and the YMCA. These organizations present a great opportunity for the community to see what you have to offer and also serve as a networking prospect for future public-speaking opportunities. More importantly, I can test out new material or tweak existing speeches and look for different audience reactions. Testing this way allows me to receive feedback that I would have never thought of myself—opinions that may be diverse and valuable.

69.

Use Pauses

We often think more quickly than we speak. As a result, sometimes our thoughts outpace our intended words, which may result in using filler words and phrases (e.g., "um," "ah," "ya know"). Before we have time to say our intended words, we may utter something of no value that can create distractions for the audience if they are plentiful. As a speaker, we need to ensure the audience gets a chance to absorb the intended content and to feel the *intended* effects. If an audience is hanging onto the words we are saying, imagine how impactful it is to hold those words or sentences in suspense. The audience will anxiously wait for the next point and have a greater appreciation when it is delivered. Let the audience take in what you have just said with a well-placed pause. Effective use of pauses allows for punchier delivery and added emphasis for your key words and points. Pauses will also allow for effective facial expressions or gestures that may garner more attention than speaking straight through without pausing.

70.

Interact with the Audience from the Beginning

There are more ways to start a speech than I can count. I previously discussed the attention-grabbing opening, and one effective way to do this is with an open-ended question for the audience to respond to, such as "Have you ever found yourself in a situation like...?" or "Can anyone give me an example when...?" Many speakers have an audience respond to a question in unison, as a group response can be full of energy if you have the right delivery and the right audience (e.g., size, demographics). For example, "When I say ____, you say ____." In these cases, the speaker is breaking the invisible wall that sometimes gets built between speaker and audience. The key is to engage the audience so that they feel like a part of the presentation. The success of the presentation grows exponentially when the audience gets into it from the very beginning, whether mentally or physically or by having the speaker grab their attention.

Once you have their attention, you must maintain audience engagement to keep the momentum as the presentation progresses. There are several ways to ensure that your audience remains committed to your message through their own involvement. Depending on the type of presentation, you may want to provide key points or facts highlighted on a handout for people to absorb and take away. Another way is to provide a fill-in-the-blank answer sheet for your participants to complete during the presentation to reinforce the message. People learn in many ways; however, the more engagement you get early on in a presentation, the greater the chance of information retention.

71.

Control the Environment

You get to the venue, get out of your car, walk straight to the podium, *and begin your talk.* I'm hoping this is not the typical way things happen before a speaking event. The important point to consider is what you, the speaker, are doing ahead of time to maximize a positive experience by controlling the speaking environment. Are you giving yourself ample time to gain a comfort level with the room so you feel in control? Your confidence level will increase when you know that the stage, the room, and the layout are to your satisfaction.

What about some of the other details that may need to be considered? Do you know where the temperature gauges are, and are you able to control them? Will you have control of the lights and the seating? When you have the chance to control the environment, you need to do so. As previously mentioned about audio-visual aspects of your presentation, you should check out the equipment, and you should also understand the acoustics. Is there an echo, and will everyone be able to hear you? When you walk around, do you find any parts of the stage that creak and might distract the audience? What about the lighting? Are bright lights blinding you? Is there a dimmer so that if the lights have to go lower, the room is not too dark?

Have you walked around the room and absorbed the potential

views from all areas? I remember a speech competition in which there was an odd, circular row of chairs around one side of the stage. This forced the outlying audience members to strain to see around poles if they wanted to see me when I was on certain parts of the stage, and also impacted where I placed my props. Fortunately, this preparation allowed me to know exactly where I would set up to ensure I maximized the audience experience visually.

When you look out into the audience, what do you see? Are there rows of seats, or are there tables? Is the seating conducive to your needs? If you encourage note-taking, will tables be more useful? When you interact with the audience, do you have them jumping out of their seats? If so, how does this play into the current set-up? Will tables cause more face-to-face side conversations that may take away from your presentation? Each speaker has his or her own preference, but you should set expectations ahead of time and get there early to make sure the set-up is what you want. As important as it is to arrange ahead of time with the organizer before the event, I have learned that things will happen that leave you scrambling if you haven't gotten there ahead of time. When you control what you can with the environment, the experience will be better for everyone.

72.

Minimize Distractions

As part of preparing with the organizer, you need to understand the anticipated timing of your presentation. Will your performance be during a meal, where glass and silverware will be clanking all around you? As follow up to the control-your-environment section, this is a critical detail to account for; if you know that a meal is immediately before or after your speech, make every effort to avoid the time when the food will be served. Wait staff moving around will inevitably distract the audience.

Will you be speaking in a classroom or similar setting, where papers may be shuffling throughout your talk? If you are in a classroom, you do have some control by setting the appropriate expectations. For example, you may let the audience know that you will stop and announce when key notes should be taken. In some cases, you may even announce that you will supply take-away notes after the session, so that the audience can sit back and relax. Again, speaker preference is important regarding what expectations you set with your audience. Use what works best for you and the type of audience you are working with. The key is to reduce the factors that can throw you off your game by anticipating as many distractions ahead of time and taking the time to mitigate or eliminate them.

73.

Find a Stage, Any Stage

Whether it is a big stage, little stage, or a small or large podium, put yourself in a setting where you are looking out on a grand room or audience. This is all about building your comfort and confidence level. Continue to find different venues to do your presentations in, and try not to get so comfortable with the same room and set-up for practice time; you don't want to get so comfortable in your practice routine and location that you will get thrown off when you are not in it. A variety of settings will get you more comfortable and enable you to present anywhere in all types of settings. In addition to increased confidence about presenting in different locations, you will start to get a feel for your own preferences for seating and room layout.

Find a stage—any stage. This includes your car, your house, and anywhere you feel there is a way to practice your presentation. On more than one occasion people have looked strangely at me while I was walking the dog, flying on an airplane, waiting in a long line, or driving down the road, as they saw me practicing. *Everywhere* can and should be your stage. I have even practiced in front of my dental hygienist in the waiting room for my bi-annual cleaning. If you gained confidence to present in front of strangers or in odd settings, imagine how good you will feel when you are in a more contained environment.

74.

Get Evaluated

Whether it was anxiously waiting for my grades in school, my performance assessments at work, or my formal speech evaluations with Toastmasters, I have learned the value of the gift of feedback; it is a constant process that should never stop. As a speaker, you need to get evaluations from your audience. It is also important to get them *immediately,* while they are fresh in people's minds. You must have thick skin, because even the best speakers get critical feedback.

We should ask for evaluations because we care. We care about getting better, and we care that our messages are getting through to the audience simply and memorably. We should be looking for trends and patterns. Be careful not to get locked into one comment or particular score; however, take each comment and score as a learning opportunity, and ask yourself what you did right and what can be improved. If you videotaped the event, you can have a targeted approach to what the evaluators may have been saying. If not, revisit in your mind what sections of the presentation the evaluations may be referencing, and take action to get better.

If I am not in position for a formal evaluation, I still make it a habit to ask attendees what they thought of the presentation afterwards. The questions shouldn't be, "Did you like it?" They should be more open-ended: "What was your favorite part?" and "If I could improve one or two things, what would they be?" Your self-esteem should never take a beating after an evaluation. However, your self-improvement antennae should be perked up. Your payback comes in the form of an even better presentation for your next audience.

75.

Use Notes — or Don't

Can or should a speaker use notes—yes or no? The answer no one wants to hear is, "It depends," but that is the answer. The variables include the location, the room set-up, and the length of the presentation. If you are in a Toastmasters speech contest, for example, you will always lose points for even potentially distracting the audience with paper or note cards in your hands. If you are speaking from a lectern, it makes sense to have notes to reference. Notice that I said "reference," not "read verbatim." Even if you stand on the stage away from the lectern, you can always slowly move back when you need to reference some material or begin the transition to a new subject. Some speakers like to use smaller note cards. Note cards are fine as long as they are not too distracting or become a focal point. A lot of the reaction from the audience is contingent on how much and how often you use your notes. If you have a teleprompter, that is a different story, but it is still important to give the impression to your audience that the words are flowing and not being read.

Most speakers tend to shy away from full-size paper, since it typically makes noise when shuffled and can be cumbersome. I have heard of having an outline on a poster board or flip chart visible to the speaker but not to the audience (in the back of the room or off to the side). In fact, although I mentioned above not to use notes if in a contest, I once wrote a discreet key word that I kept forgetting on a prop (that could not be seen). Ironically, I never once referenced it in the middle of the contest, but knowing it was there boosted my confidence level. What's important is that the audience gets your message without the notes getting in the way. Never become fully dependent on, and read directly from, your notes (if you use them). However, you may be surprised to hear that most experienced speakers do use some form of notes for presentations typically over ten minutes. If you have prepared your presentation correctly, and you use your notes effectively, the presentation becomes more about bringing messages, stories, and facts alive than, "Did I say the exact words verbatim from the sheet or notes in front of me?"

76.

Know Your Speech Rate

Do you know how many words you speak per minute or how long it takes you to get through a speech of single-lined text on a piece of paper? What is your typical pace? And, why are these questions relevant? Understanding how quickly you speak will assist you as you are writing out your presentation. It will help you as you move from your outline to the actual text to see if you have enough or too much material. Your speaking speed will vary once you start practicing out loud because you will build in strategic pauses, movement on the podium, and gestures that will impact your timing and speed.

I didn't realize early in my speaking career that I was inadvertently counting my words. I knew that for a five to seven-minute speech (based on the size-ten font I typically use), I could have a full page plus one paragraph on the second page and stay within seven minutes. This was early in my public-speaking experience, because I depended more on my notes. After learning to memorize similar-length speeches, I found I couldn't have that extra paragraph because I was getting better at responding to audience reactions and at using pauses for effect; the timing of my speeches changed based on my experience level. I have settled in to around 800 to 850 words for a seven-minute speech, after I also account for anticipated audience reactions (about 115 to

125 words per minute). There is obvious variation based on the topic and delivery, but I know instantly when writing speeches if I have too much or too little based on the allotted time. I now know that I need to eliminate thirty words to cut down my time by about fifteen seconds. Once you settle into a good routine, you will become very familiar with your speech-writing timing needs.

77.

Memorize the Speech — or Don't

Y ou have outlined and then written out the speech, and it is ready to practice. I convinced myself that, as I was terrible at remembering names and other things, I would also have trouble remembering speeches without notes. It took plenty of practice and new tips along the way, but now I feel confident in my ability to remember my speeches. Below are some key tips:

• Go back and look at the outline to determine if the beginning, body, and conclusion are logically arranged. I have found that some simple re-arrangement of sentences can make all the difference in my ability to memorize.

• Smooth out the speech to give it a more even flow if you find yourself stumbling during transition points. The flow and rhythm are important.

• Don't mumble the speech under your breath. You must be loud and proud. Everything is a live rehearsal and will help your retention and allow you to figure out better words to use. You will be surprised how different your speech sounds from what you intended when you originally wrote it.

• Learn in small increments. I begin by setting a goal of memorizing a paragraph a day. Before work, I invest time going over the paragraph to remember it. On my commute home from work, which takes about thirty minutes, I try to recall the most recent portion of the speech I worked on. By the end of the day, I have the baseline of the paragraph down. The next day, I reinforce the first paragraph and begin the second. I continue this progressive approach until I remember the entire passage. You should note that if you choose not to memorize the entire speech, you should at least invest the time to know your material inside and out. Many experienced people in the field of public speaking argue the wisdom of memorizing entire speeches. Some argue that the presentation becomes too acted or prescribed. I will leave it up to each individual as to how they want to prepare their work. What is typically agreed on is the importance of memorizing a strong opening and conclusion, with a laser focus pointed on the key message and topics that must be stated within the presentation to define the success of the speech.

• Visualize the speech in your head. With the small increments noted above, you can begin to visualize the speech order based on key words and sentence structures. Visualizing is slightly different from memorizing because, to some extent, you are living the speech by thinking about words, places you want to be on stage, and flow.

• Use gestures to accompany your words, and use your body to guide your mind. I have almost forgotten words many times, but built strong gesture routines and habits in which my arms and hands prompted me with word memories.

• Incorporate alliteration. This shouldn't be overdone, but it's always a great tool to throw in occasionally (e.g., *h*elpless, *h*omeless, and *h*urting…).

• Practice in different surroundings so you don't get too comfortable in one forum. For example, as noted above, I often practice while driving home from work. Afterwards, I am always shocked the first time I stand up and practice it. I always seem thrown off simply by standing the first time.

• Even if the speech isn't perfect, practice with other people or a video camera. This added pressure builds your concentration level.

• Use videotape to help underline some trouble spots for remembering. This comes back to being able to visualize yourself on the stage.

• Then practice, practice, practice. You can never practice too much.

78.

Listen Better

Toastmasters' club meetings emphasize the importance of speech evaluations and designate certain individuals to listen for proper grammar and filler words. Personally and professionally, I knew I needed to be a better listener, because I had a reputation for periodically speaking over people as they spoke. The habit was not to be disrespectful, but was often an attempt to rush out my own words while they were fresh in my head. However, I had never correlated the importance of public speaking with listening. With a larger group of people, especially during question-and-answer sessions, Toastmasters training gave me more restraint in the business environment. I began to actively listen to the questions and then thoughtfully try to answer them.

In addition to Q&A sessions, I started listening not only with my ears, but with my eyes. My observation skills were becoming honed because I needed to adjust to audience reactions during my presentations, whether it was by seeing sighs, yawns, closed eyes, or even no reaction at all. Altering presentation and delivery to adapt to audience needs, even in mid-stream, helps not only with the present speech, but with future versions of that same speech. Additionally, becoming a better listener has made me a better communicator all around. This more holistic communication approach, including speaking and listening, has increased my confidence and made me more adept in the business setting.

79.

Assume Nothing

You can't assume anything prior to speaking. You need to do your homework, even if you are asked to give a "quick" status update on a project to your manager and a group of his or her peers. You have the right and obligation to ask how long you are expected to speak for, who will be there, who else may be speaking, and if there will be a question-and-answer session. Even though questions are typically asked at this kind of event, it's still worth checking. Wouldn't it be better to know ahead of time if the questions will be asked during the presentation or after the presentation?

You must also confirm the time and place. I know it sounds obvious, but I was embarrassed once when I showed up for a speaking engagement at a local Kiwanis Club and saw that there was another speaker. I had failed to re-confirm the time with the sponsor. The sponsor didn't reach out to me, but I hold myself accountable for assuming I was confirmed after the first email I received. Even if you think you know the answers, ask questions anyway to ensure that everyone is on the same page. Clarifying and confirming are key tools in your speaking arsenal.

80.

Avoid Cold Transitions

When you are moving from the introduction to the main body of the speech and then to the conclusion, make sure you use warm transitions. You can't jolt the audience with an eye-opening introduction about aliens landing on earth and then go into the body of your speech as if alien landings are completely normal by sharing examples of how the aliens are getting along just fine on this planet. I was working on a speech about my shy daughter's triumphant solo chorus performance. The message was about how her bravery of stepping out on that stage alone led me to alter my perspective of a special needs co-worker based on how he bravely participated in the Special Olympics. Early versions of the speech received consistent feedback from friends and family that the transition from my daughter to the Special Olympics athlete was too cold. I needed more character description to paint the picture of him as an individual first, before jumping in with both feet.

You need to add some semblance of a transition that enables the listener to go back in time and put all the pieces of the story together. We can effectively go from the attention-grabbing introduction into a smooth changeover into the body of the presentation. Back to the alien example: if you add small bites for the audience to chew on, such as, "After an exhaustive struggle, the aliens found common ground with the earthlings by…," the audience can find the connection. I sometimes hear this referenced as getting the string and pulling it all the way through. I actually found two effective transition versions that worked on the Special Olympics speech. First, I used a pondering open-ended question for the audience about potential catalysts for change in their lives. Second, I add a simple phrase that said, "A few days after my daughter's triumph adjusted my lens on beauty…." Both changes received positive feedback relating to a smoother transition. With a warmer jump between topics, stories, and key points, the audience will be able to follow the flow more easily. Smooth transitions allow easier understanding of the organization and content of the speech.

81.

Manage Q&A Basics

Many presentations end with question-and-answer sessions. Here are some of the basics to remember:

• Notice I said the *end*; outside of direct attempts to solicit audience responses and intentional open-ended parts of the presentation, I recommend saving questions for the end, to avoid jeopardizing the flow and taking away from later material.

• Save your final key take-away points and/or message for after the Q&A so you can dictate the final messaging.

• Repeat questions back to the audience to ensure they are understood and for people who may not have heard them (this also buys you some time to formulate answers).

• Avoid rambling; answers should be clear and concise. Yes, this seems obvious, but it is a critical skill to master.

• Don't guess. Offer to get back to the overall audience or to the person who asked the question, or even look for a subject expert in the audience who may be better suited to answer. It is better to have the right answer than guess incorrectly. The creditability that you earned throughout the presentation is still at risk during Q&A time.

• Be an attentive listener. You should make every effort to not cut off the question because you anticipate the rest of it. Give the person asking as much courtesy as he or she has given you.

Stir Emotion

82.

Live in the Present

With dread, I waited in the lobby an hour before the biggest speech competition of my life. For the first time, I had the opportunity to compete against seven other speakers for the chance to represent our district in the Toastmasters World Semi-finals International Speech Competition. Unfortunately, I hadn't learned yet that the words "fun" and "public speaking," could be used in the same sentence.

I asked Joey Grondin, the eventual contest winner, what he did to relax. He simply said, "Live in the present." He went on to say that this moment would never come again, so why not enjoy it? If you grasp hold of the now, then the audience will get caught up in the moment, too. So, I stopped worrying about making mistakes and basked in the moment I had on the podium. When I did, in fact, make a large mistake by having an awkward pause while I tried to remember what I wanted to say next, I watched the audience feel my emotions and provide the encouragement and support I needed to ultimately have the most fun I ever had in my early speaking career.

83.

Leave the Audience with the Upside

Many inspirational messages start with hitting rock bottom or some type of roadblock. We want the audience to experience the downs and ups of the message with us. Even as we relate to the audience with a phrase such as, "We have all experienced hard times or the heartache of…," we need to ensure we carry the audience back out of the valley to the uplifting high point. It may seem obvious, but sometimes the despair is deeper than we think. We must be conscientious about holding the hand of the audience and pulling them along with us to the final inspirational message.

84.

Know the Difference between Motivation and Inspiration

Inspiration and motivation are often used interchangeably. As a speaker, you must understand the difference in order to achieve the full effect of what you are trying to convey.

An inspirational message typically takes the audience on a journey. It often is a part of the individual speaker's personal trials and tribulations. The inspirational ride is driven primarily through an emotional connection to the audience. However, motivational speeches carry with them a take-away or a specific request of the audience. You'll try to persuade the audience to take some kind of action, whether to change their ways—such as eating habits, for example—or to accomplish something, such as running a marathon. Simply sharing your own personal successes with an audience is not being specific enough to motivate them to join in.

If you want an audience to be motivated, you need to tell them or ask them to take a specific action. Staying with the example of eating habits, you may want to ask the audience to start reading the labels when they get home, counting calories against the recommended intake, and incorporating the appropriate amount of fruits and vegetables into their diets. You must convey specifics if you truly want to motivate a positive change.

85.

Be Funny, Even Though I'm Not

I used to do a monthly presentation at work for newer employees. The topic was often financial fraud, which can be a scary or fascinating topic, depending on how the audience relates to it. I tried to have fun with it to ease the mood and hold the audience members' attention. I started to receive consistent feedback that I was funny and engaging on this potentially complicated topic. I went home and told my wife and she simply said sarcastically, in the way only a spouse could, "You're not funny."

I have retold this story many times and always seem to get some laughs. I do have my funny moments, and it is important to inject humor into your presentations, when possible. Not every presentation is required to have humor, but if you can find a way to appropriately add it in, even during serious presentations, you will give your audience a release and the chance to get more involved in the presentation.

86.

Look Around for Humor

My personality leans toward being more serious than funny. I have my moments, but I have to work hard to get some laughs. I have concluded that I will never be a stand-up comedian, but I have had more fun with myself, and the audience, once I stopped putting so much effort into being funny. I found all I had to do was remember to just look around me. We are surrounded by humor.

Self-deprecating humor is always a winner and usually won't offend the audience. It can be fun to go back and remember funny and embarrassing stories from your childhood, from school, or from work. You may even begin to chuckle when you unleash the repressed memories. How many times have you sat around the dinner table and rehashed humorous stories with family and friends? After dinner, jot down some notes to help you remember, and throw them in that folder or file.

Look around you. Have you ever passed a sign that made you laugh? I have learned that humor isn't all about one-liners or long, drawn-out stories. The simple stories can get a great reaction. For example, my wife was driving down the road when my fourteen-year-old daughter, at the time, asked her about an old building they had just passed. My wife said that it was an old topless bar. This is the part in the story where people start getting very concerned about appropriateness. You can relax. My daughter asked, "What did they do when it rained?" We are surrounded with funny life moments.

87.

Find the Funny Soon

Comedians use quick-hitting humor and one-liners because they don't want to lose the audience. They work on timing and delivery to get the biggest laughs. I learned that not everything a speaker says needs to be side-splittingly funny. Going for a few chuckles can be just as entertaining to an audience. You simply need to know what your audience wants and expects.

Once you determine this, you can develop your humorous stories. As with a quick-hitting comedic set-up, you must get to the humorous part of the story sooner rather than later. I have watched speeches crash as the audience knew something funny was coming but it took too long to get to the punch. I was involved in a humorous-speech competition, and four of the first seven contestants went several minutes into a five-to seven-minute speech before they delivered their first laugh. Don't get me wrong. My fellow competitors were hilarious once they got rolling, but they had unfortunately lost many of the judges and audience members, who were expecting the funny parts sooner. Don't let the audience wait too long to laugh.

88.

Let the Audience Know It's Okay to Laugh

I was practicing a very serious speech for the first time in front of a co-worker. It was very personal and emotional. However, in a couple of spots I attempted to add some levity, to ease the seriousness of the message. I saw no reaction to my attempts at humor. After the speech, I asked my co-worker if it was inappropriate, ill-timed, or just not funny. She said she thought it was funny but she wasn't sure, given the heavy weight of the message, if she was *allowed* to laugh.

The speaker needs to give some indication, whether it is a wink or a smile or some other kind of non-verbal or verbal "permission," for the audience to come along on their journey. A well-placed pause, for example, with an emerging smile may be enough to connect with the audience and let them know it's okay to laugh.

89.

Exude Energy — It's Contagious

Have you ever had a presenter stand in front of you and lethargically say, "Hi, my name is John, and I'm really excited to be here." My first thought is always a sarcastic, "It looks like it." What am I supposed to look forward to as someone in the audience? Energy is contagious, and the audience needs to feel the passion and enthusiasm you want to share with them. Your ability to genuinely exude your hunger and to motivate and inspire your audience will get the group hungry to receive your message. Words without energy are just words without meaning—until you bring them to life.

90.

Be Sincere —
It Means More Than Words

You can have the most thoughtful and powerful words ever written, but if they don't come from your heart, they will land flat. Always give your audience credit for the ability to see through speakers who may not believe in what they're talking about. Your own credibility is at stake, and your ability to show the real you, including your personality, values, and beliefs, will always connect with an audience.

At times you may want to exaggerate a point, to set the tone or to get the audience to visualize the message. Many public-speaking books say that it is acceptable to stretch the facts a little to ensure that the significance is grasped. However, even with tall tales or embellished stories, you have to show that you, yourself, believe them and can execute them with burning passion because they are coming from your heart and soul. An audience may not always agree with your points or message, but they must always believe it is the real you.

91.

Emphasize Physical Aspects in the Speech

We hear "public speaking" and obviously think about the spoken words. We invest a lot of time as speakers in selecting the perfect word for the perfect situation. As we prepare and practice, we should remember to work on the *complete* package, beyond memorizing the words and vocalizing. In our speech development, we sometimes lose the physical aspects of the speech that can make the presentation come alive.

Physical aspects of the speech include facial expressions and gestures. Imagine a speaker sharing a "shocking" story with a blank look on his or her face. Like a punch line in comedy, you need your face and body to emphasize the emotions of the words to bring them alive. In the "shocking" example, you would probably expect wide eyes or a gaping mouth. Let the audience share the experience with you. Your facial expressions may not even need words if your feelings can be seen and related to by the audience.

Gestures are also important in moving the speech along, and you must remember both the importance of timing and the naturalness of the movements. You don't want your movements to come across as staged or prescribed. Although practicing the gestures to get them to the point where you want them is imperative as you put the whole package together, you do not want them to come across as acting. The physical aspects of the speech are one more way to look at the speech process holistically.

92.

Go Big

You might ask the audience for a response and tentatively raise your hand in the hopes that they will, too. However, the tips of your own fingers may not even go above your head. How will the audience react? They, too, will be reluctant to raise their hands because they are taking their cues from you. Go big with your gestures. You should let it out like you mean it. This doesn't mean going so far outside of your own comfort level that you are not being genuine, but understand that the audience needs to see the energy and enthusiasm of an effective gesture.

The audience wants to get the most out of the physical and nonverbal aspects of your speech. If you are giving a sly smile, don't make it quick. Give a pause with the slow emergence of a smile so the audience gets the full effect. A friend of mine who is an experienced swimmer always talks about the full extension of the fingertips through the water. The same concept should apply here with your gestures, vocals, and any other pieces of the speech that can stir the audience. In a speech, if you mention being a sprinter in a race, take a few quick, bursting steps. You should fully embrace the emotion you want to evoke in the audience. The audience should definitely know how you are feeling and what you are doing—don't make them guess or assume. Their ability to view and immediately grasp your every move will enhance their engagement, involvement, and understanding.

93.

Turn Off the Lights and Watch Them Snooze

Speakers turn off the lights for many reasons. One of the obvious is that the need to see presentation slides clearly. As you have read, you will want to minimize your dependence on slides, when possible, and also have the font big enough that the audience doesn't need to strain, which may, in turn, allow for just dimming the lights or even keeping them on altogether. Personally, I turned off the lights in my early public-speaking experience because of the blotchiness on my neck and face that I didn't want seen. I also suspect that I didn't want to look the audience in the eyes. I might also add that I often accomplished that mission because audience members' eyelids would close when the darkness came. Just think back to any school experience when the teacher turned down the lights to show a movie, for example, in class.

When the lights go down, the comfort level of the audience goes up. Regardless of how engaging you are, you will always fight audience drowsiness. If you do need to project a presentation, do it in short spurts, or simply turn the lights down, but not off. If there is background lighting, try to use that. If you must turn off the lights, try using interactive responses from the group to keep them focused on the message. Don't disengage the audience by putting them in the dark.

94.

Share Emotions

Wॺe all laugh, cry, and even scream when we see something scary. Have you ever noticed that laugh tracks are included in many sitcoms on television because laughter is contagious? Everyone does it. David Brooks, the 1990 Toastmasters World Champion of Public Speaking, shared a story on his "Dave's Top Ten Techniques Every Speaker Should Know" CD about an article in the *Austin American Statesman* (LM Boyd's "Trivia" column) that mentioned that we all share the same emotions: happiness, sadness, anger, surprise, disgust, and fear. As we search high and low for stories that can hit the mark, maybe we don't have to look so hard. Simple stories can touch one of the emotions listed above and are guaranteed to relate to the audience in some way. As you share your emotions, you will see members of the audience thinking of a similar time when they felt the same emotion. Sharing emotions instantly connects you to the audience.

95.

Personalize the Presentation

I once watched a presenter attempt to give a salient argument about the dangers of texting and driving. The intended message was to persuade us to practice safe driving and to pass this important message on to others. However, the speaker referenced a local story read out of a newspaper as the focal point of the message. As sad a story as it was when she related the fact that someone had died, the speech felt like it was missing something: the personal touch. I kept asking myself, "How was the speaker connected to the message? Did they have a friend or a family member affected?" I needed to know what made her so passionate about the message.

Not every story needs to be a tear jerker. In fact, I am glad that the speaker was not directly impacted by this example. However, the audience is left guessing when a message does not have the personal appeal that makes it our own. The stories that make up your life will have the greatest impact on any audience because they are unique and new. They will tend to connect genuinely to the hearts and minds of the audience because these stories sincerely come from your heart and mind, with stirring personal emotion, not just emphasized words.

96.

Jump in Feet First

Ever hear a presentation start with, "How's everyone doing today?" or another generic opening? How about when a significant amount of time is spent listing out things that will be discussed during the event? Have you ever watched the painful beginnings of a presentation when a generic introduction droned on and on? The audience warm-up, in some cases, may become a cool-down where you lose them before you even begin the foundation of your presentation.

Ed Tate, in a presentation at the District 45 2010 Fall Conference talked about jumping immediately into the presentation content. If you had an effective introduction given about you (I hope you wrote it yourself), you should jump right away into the substance, since you should already be set up. The audience is there for the presentation messages, not the generic introductions. Since I started jumping right in, I have found audiences to be more engaged earlier in the presentation because I grabbed their attention from the beginning. A strong introduction is important, and stating what material you will be discussing is important, but the key is to keep the introductions concise and meaningful, and integrate the agenda *after* the audience is fully engaged.

97.

Understand that Learning
Is a Process, Not an Event

Some gravitational pull may have led you to this book. Whether you felt your stomach drop in an important business presentation or you have a pending proposal you need to make, regardless of the reason, you have dedicated yourself to improving your public speaking. You have taken an exciting step toward your ultimate success.

You should be cautiously optimistic that your journey is just beginning, regardless of your level as a public speaker. Remember that even when your important presentation is over, the public speaking is not. The event may be over, but the process continues. The art of public speaking, and your progress, is ever evolving. The learning process needs constant attention and refinement. It does not happen overnight, but it does happen when you continue to take action. You have already made the tough choice to improve—that was an action. Now, you should make sure that your commitment is strong. Continue to build long-lasting habits that will become your foundation and baseline to work from.

Learning is a process, not an event. Some of you may have some natural ability, and some may not. However, the ability to move forward and improve only happens after you cross over the threshold past the inertia, and then keep your advancement toward success alive.

98.

Be Inspirational, Not Loud

Have you ever watched an inspirational speaker whose sole ability to inspire seemed to come from his loud voice? As you flip through television channels you are bound to land on a station where someone is trying to sell you something or "inspire you" to give away your money somehow. Much of this is driven through the volume and urgency of the voices saying, "Do it now!" The urgency of the "now" builds the excitement, and that excitement often raises the volume of the speaker. I'm not saying that the loud voices are yelling; they do have a constant tone and pitch that often maintains this sense of urgency through the higher volume.

I have been in situations when I know that the speaker's goal was to motivate or inspire me, but I felt more discomfort—or in some cases boredom— since there was too much constant volume. Many times in these cases, I have found very little vocal variety, so the speech becomes monotonous. In some cases, a speaker's inspirational message is simply about repeating the same words or phrases over and over. Although some repetition is encouraged to ensure the message sticks with an audience, using the same boisterous tone may get old without any vocal variety. I find my mind starting to wander when the loud voice gives me a feeling of being talked at, as opposed to being talked to or talked with.

Inspiration can come from different types of speakers. Many speakers have caught and kept my attention by effectively varying their voice and pitch. Some spend a lot of time in the higher-volume state, and I am all right with that because they periodically bring it down. Most importantly, they have a *message* that has connected with me and has maintained my attention, not simply because they had a loud voice. Loud may get your attention, but will it *maintain* that attention?

Whether you are introverted, extroverted, loud, or soft, realize that inspiration can come from all types of speakers. The delivery is one factor to ensure your effectiveness, and having an important message for the audience to take away is another. Have you captured the hearts and minds of the people you are interacting with? You can connect in so many different ways with the audience. Just be confident in knowing that you are connecting.

99.

Use Quotations

Using quotations can be complex. When, where, and how to effectively incorporate them into your speech can be tough. When it becomes tough, try to determine whether you are forcing it for the sake of a quotation that you like. Ask yourself a few questions: Will the audience like it as much as I do? Does it have a connection to the message I am sending? Is it simple enough to say in a couple of sentences?

I have seen too many speeches in which a quotation was too complex for the simple message being delivered. In some cases, I have heard quotations that were hard for the audience to keep up with. One of my favorite quotations is, "Change is inevitable, growth is optional," by John C. Maxwell. I first saw it taped up in my office. This quotation has stuck with me for many years. It resonates as a strong business quote, especially in an ever-evolving corporate environment. It is simple and easily relatable to many audiences. The impact can be felt in so many places.

The most effective quotations seem to be the most straightforward. "Many people die with the music still in them," by Oliver Wendell Holmes, has its own effortlessness that can be applied in multiple scenarios. Take the audience on a journey with you by using quotations. Make the message memorable and simple—simply make sure the timing is right and that your quotation fits just so. Recognize that quotations should be used to set the tone or reinforce your message. You should try not to jam them into a presentation because you feel obligated. Keep a list of attention-grabbing quotes. Keep a folder of your favorites for future presentations. When you are looking for the right words, go back and reference the folder, to see how a favorite quotation can spice up your presentation.

Note: Whether you are using a quotation, comic strip, music, or anything else that is not your own material, be sure to cite the source and originator for appropriate credit. Please also ensure you are not infringing on copyrights or protected material.

100.

Move with Purpose

Some speakers wander the stage with what seems like no purpose. They walk back and forth across the front of the stage or simply meander from place to place. This can distract the audience. In fact, early in my speaking career, I paced back and forth to get rid of my nervous energy. This wasn't a bad idea, considering how much my legs would shake, so I wasn't sure if I could stand in one spot, anyway. I was given some feedback recommending that I cut back on some of my movement. I misinterpreted the feedback and stood in the same spot. I no longer distracted the audience, but I appeared even more upright and uptight than when I was pacing. I needed to find a happy medium if I wanted to get my messages across to the audience.

I began to study other speakers' movement. I found out that the effective ones casually walked the stage but were not pacing. They stopped on key points and the movement had a nice, even flow. They always seemed to know how to navigate the stage without distracting the audience or enabling us to predict their every move. The nature of the walk was the fundamental difference. The movement had purpose, but remained as natural as walking down the street. The casual-walk-with-friends approach solved my need to walk the stage to release my nervous energy, and at the same time made me appear as if we were just having a conversation while walking the dog.

101.

Use Your Voice as a Tool

Your voice has variety, so use it. Whether you are trying to project volume or are making soft-spoken points to reach the hearts of the audience, you can use the full range of what your voice has to offer. I have been watching the growth of one of my Toastmasters club members. In a speech about a scary movie, he described himself, "Screaming like a little girl." When he first started practicing, his squeal was soft and constrained. He was coached to let it all out with a mighty, high-pitched noise. His new approach was uninhibited and achieved his purpose. The audience reacted with a jolt.

You can use various pitches to put yourself in the moment and even use different voices if you are speaking as a character or a third party for further impacts. You don't have to be a full-blown actor or actress to spice up your presentations with different emotions brought to life with your voice. Additionally, you can use pace to your advantage to convey the urgency of a story or slow it down to set the stage for the audience. For example, audience members will almost feel themselves getting exhausted when they hear you breathing heavily as if you have just run a marathon. Use your voice as a tool and watch your own effectiveness soar.

102.

Keep It Simple

Write speeches that are well-matched with your personality, your education, your style, and your comfort level. I consider myself oversimplified in some cases, and that's the way I like it. When I have attempted to sound smart or use big words, I have found a growing sense of discomfort and unease during the presentation. As speakers, we should make every effort to use descriptive words that paint the picture of what we are trying to say, but our word choice shouldn't deviate too far from who we are normally. Newscasts or effective writing on the Internet intentionally uses shorter sentences with simple words to grab the most attention (funny how I almost used "garner" instead of "grab"—that would have been too ironic). Your credibility comes from people getting to know who you are as a speaker personally. If you start using words that don't typically come from your mouth, they will sound forced and fake, and potentially will hurt the credibility you are working so hard to gain.

103.

Share Your Vulnerability

We have all had an argument, we have all made mistakes, and we have all been nervous. We all share some common ground, whether it's our background, stories, or situations. When you share those moments, they will resonate instantly with lots of audiences. Many inexperienced speakers are too cautious in their approach to sharing their vulnerabilities and mistakes with the crowd. In my early speaking career, I kept things at a high level; I could have almost been described as vanilla in my early speeches. They were surface only and didn't dive into who I really was. It was only after I started to open my soul and share personal stories that I began to hold the interest of my audiences.

I have seen speakers who have hung on tight to intimate details that would most likely hit home with the audience. I know that these speakers had something poignant to be shared, but it remained bottled up. If the topic made sense, and it was still appropriate to share in order to connect with the audience, why wouldn't they? We are sometimes too self-conscious to let it all out, but your success with the audience almost *depends* on doing so. You may even find a little therapy for yourself—at least I did. I have obviously included in this book many of the mistakes I have made as a speaker; what you should also see is the journey and learning that followed. Lead your own audience through to your final destination—your take-away message. An effective way to get there is with moving, personal, relatable stories that leave you exposed enough to hit the audience right in their hearts and head.

References

Bailey, Keith and Karen Leland. *Public Speaking in an Instant: 60 Ways to Stand Up and Be Heard.* Franklin Lakes, NJ: Career Press, 2009.

Brooks, David. *Dave's Top Ten Techniques Every Speaker Should Know.* CD, 2004.

CTRN: Changes That's Right Now, March 16, 2012. www.changethatsrightnow.com.

Metzer, D. www.owningthestage.com. "*What is stage fright, and what causes it.*" September 2, 2008. Accessed March 13, 2012.

Davidson, Jeff. *The Complete Guide to Public Speaking.* Hoboken, NJ: John Wiley & Sons, 2003.

Dowis, Richard. *The Lost Art of the Great Speech.* New York: Amacon, 1999.

Esposito, Janet. *Getting Over Stage Fright—A New Approach to Resolving Your Fear of Public Speaking and Performing.* St. Louis, MO: Love Your Life Publishing, Inc., 2009.

Esposito, Janet. *In the SpotLight—Overcome Your Fear of Public Speaking and Performing.* Bridgeport, CT: In the SpotLight, LLC, 2000.

Grondin, Joey. *Developing Your Signature*. CD, 2009.

Humes, James C. *Speak like Churchill, Stand Like Lincoln: 21 Powerful Secrets of History's Greatest Speakers*. Three Rivers Press, 2002.

Numoroff, Laura. *If You Give a Mouse a Cookie*. HarperCollins Publishers, 1985.

Smith, Scott S. *The Everything Public Speaking Book: Deliver a Winning Presentation Every Time!*, Avon, MA: Adams Media, 2008.

Theobald, Theo. *Develop Your Presentation Skills: Build Your Confidence; Be Charismatic; Give a Polished Performance*. London: Kogan Page, 2011.

Acknowledgements

My ability to speak more effectively in a public forum has directly correlated with my professional and personal success. However, I would have had no success without the many people I have crossed paths with in Toastmasters International, and professionally at Bank of America. I want to thank the countless friends who have offered their support, encouragement, and opinions. I also want to express my undying gratitude to anyone who let me run with my ideas. This appreciation includes all of the people who knew I had the potential but needed further refinement, and it also includes the speech mentors and competitors I lost to who made me (consciously or unconsciously) write, rewrite, and rewrite again to ensure that I gave nothing but the best to the audience.

I have a long way to go in my continued development and learning, but I want to thank my wife, Ellen, and my children, Meg, Erin, and Tatum, for being supportive every step of the way. I am very appreciative of the Chamberlin family (Beth, Parker, Thatcher, Abby and Henry) who unknowingly became a part of my speaking business when they fatefully agreed to listen to that one speech that has since turned into many. Their encouragement has been incredible. I want to thank my editor Jen Blood from Maine Authors Publishing for making my thoughts have more meaning. I want to recognize Polly Hall for cleaning up the little details toward the end of the editing process. Finally, I am grateful for the chance encounter with a fellow Toastmaster, and my favorite public-speaking professor, Dog Wallace, who always inspires me to extend my message to more people every time I talk to him. Thank you for the inspirational editing assistance.

About the Author

For as long as he could remember, Tom Dowd was the one who constantly felt the heat rush up through his neck and head before speaking publicly. Each time he spoke one-on-one or to hundreds of people, it was a constant reminder of his fear of speaking. Now, he only remembers this when there is a brief lapse in confidence, or he is teaching others that it doesn't matter as long as you have a message. He is sure it still happens all of the time, but it no longer takes away from what he wants to accomplish.

Tom graduated from the University of Delaware in 1990 with a Communication degree, concentrating on interpersonal and organizational communication. With over twenty years of experience in the corporate world in management and leadership roles, Tom is currently an executive at Bank of America. He has learned that his satisfaction level personally and professionally is directly correlated to his confidence level in his own abilities. He gained this confidence by being a constant learner and then a teacher. His methods go beyond surviving: he finally understood that true success comes from being self-aware, believing that change is possible, and then taking action. A major catalyst in taking action happened when Tom joined Toastmasters International in 2008, where he quickly gained success as an award-winning speaker and leader. He has won multiple speech contests at the state and regional level with humorous, impromptu, inspirational, and evaluative speech competitions. He was selected as the 2010-11 District 45 Toastmaster of the Year and is also a member of the National Speakers Association. In 2011 his expertise as a speaker, author, trainer, and coach led him to start his own business, *Thomas Dowd Professional*

Development and Coaching. Tom frequently presents to, and coaches, a wide variety of audiences ranging from students, community members, and professionals. He can be reached through his website at www.transformationtom.com. In addition to this book, he is simultaneously publishing *The Transformation of a Doubting Thomas: Growing from a Cynic to a Professional in the Corporate World.*

Tom lives in Camden, Maine, with his wife and three daughters.